DEVELOPMENT AFTER PHYSICAL ABUSE IN EARLY CHILDHOOD

A follow-up study of children on protection registers

JANE GIBBONS BERNARD GALLAGHER
CAROLINE BELL DAVID GORDON
Social Work Development Unit, University of East Anglia

STUDIES IN CHILD PROTECTION

LONDON: HMSO

First published 1995

ISBN 0 11 321790 0

Contents

List of tables

List of tables—*continued*

List of figures

Acknowledgements

In planning and carrying out the study we received help from literally hundreds of people. For reasons of confidentiality we cannot acknowledge every individual by name but we record our debts here. We thank the families who took part, generously giving their time and effort in the hope that other children and families would benefit in the long run. We are grateful to heads of school and teachers who completed questionnaires at a time when they were under particular pressure. We thank the staff in social services and voluntary agencies and in the health service who helped us in many ways.

Ms A. Booth, Mrs V. Massey and Mrs M. O'Brien (with Caroline Bell) carried out the arduous task of extracting data from social and medical records. Research assessments were carried out by Mrs W. Ricardo, Mrs M. Rowe, Mrs L. Tomlinson, Mrs V. Hamilton, Mrs K. Johnson and Mrs M. Oliver. Ms Ann Rushton trained the assessors in the use of the educational instruments. Professor R.G. Burwell allowed the research nurses to receive instruction at his growth clinic and also advised on measurements. Dr M. Blair, Dr L. Polnay and Dr T. Hutchinson advised on the use of medical records data. We thank Dr C. Elliott and Dr P. Farrell for advice on educational assessment. Other help or advice came from Dr A. Bradbury, Ms H. Bohme, Mr B. Field, Dr J. Roland, Mrs P. Steel, Mrs J. Andrews, Ms M. Collinge, Mr N. Hanson, Dr P. Keavney, Dr J. Moulton and Mrs J. Swan. We acknowledge the special help of Professor P. Mittler, Professor of Special Education, Manchester University and Professor M. Davies, head of School of Social Work at the University of East Anglia. We are grateful to Diane McCool and staff for help with computing; and to Ms A. Booth and Ms D. Barwick for outstanding word-processing services. We are grateful to Mrs Hilary Gellman, Mrs Dady Key, Ms Caroline Sutcliffe and Mrs Lynette Tomlinson for their exceptional perseverence and skill in recruiting families into the study and interviewing. Studies like this one cannot be carried out without the highly specialised and professional skill of research interviewers. We were fortunate in finding four such outstanding practitioners of the art.

The National Society for the Protection of Children offered consistent support to the project. Ms Sue Creighton, Senior Research Officer, made an important contribution through her liaison work. We acknowledge the help of the members of the project's Central Advisory Committee: Professor Sir Michael Rutter (Chair), Dr F. Bamford, Dr P. Barbor, Professor M. Beveridge, Mr C. Blakey, Ms S. Creighton, Dr C. Davies, Mr J. Harding, Dr M. Lynch, Professor P. Mittler, Mrs E. Monck, Mrs A. Parker, Mr J. Pickett, Professor I. Sinclair, Dr L. Smith, Mr N. Todd and Dr D. Quinton. We are particularly grateful to Dr Barbor for his technical and practical help, and to Dr Quinton for help in developing the children's interview as well as (with Ms P. Remon) in tracing. Elizabeth Monck (with Dr Marjorie Smith) helped in training the interviewers. Professor Rutter generously gave his time in striving to help us improve the project. Members of the Advisory Committee are not responsible for the deficiencies that remain. The study was funded by the Department of Health. We are grateful to Dr Carolyn Davies, our liaison officer. Finally we acknowledge the help of Professor Spencer Milham and the Dartington Social Research Unit in providing a forum where researchers into services for children can learn from each other.

Summary

Aims of study

In a nine to ten year follow-up of children placed on child protection registers to describe:

- the longer-term consequences of physical ill-treatment
- whether the circumstances of the original abuse had any predictive power in relation to children's safety and outcomes in the longer term
- the extent of life changes during the follow-up period and their effects
- the family relationships of the children in the present
- the protective and supportive services provided by the key agency and whether they influenced outcomes
- the consquences of placement in substitute families. *(Introduction)*

Methods

The total (Index) sample included all 170 children under five placed on registers operated by the NSPCC in two areas during the course of one year. Each Index case had a paired Comparison child who attended the same school and was matched for gender, age and area of residence. Outcome measures were applied to both groups: physical growth; parent and teacher ratings of behaviour; standard cognitive tests; children's own accounts of friendship problems and their scores on fears and depression questionnaires.

165 out of 170 Index children were traced to an address in Britain and 144 (85%) took part with their Comparison pairs. *(Chapters 1&9)*

Results

Although Index and Comparison families had a similar social class distribution, Index families were poorer, more often headed by a lone parent and more mobile. *(Chapter 1)*

Allowing for social status differences, Index children showed more behaviour problems at home and school, had more friendship problems and scored lower on some cognitive tests. There were no differences between Index and Comparison children in physical growth or self-rated depression and fears. Using the 'best' discrimination, the likelihood of the difference between Index and Comparison groups being due to chance was 1 in 10 000. However, there was considerable overlap, with about a fifth of the Comparison children displaying serious behavioural and academic problems and a similar proportion of Index children largely free from problems. 22% of the Index children were classified as having a generally good outcome on the measures of behaviour, emotions and cognitive performance; 42% as having a poor outcome; and 36% as intermediate. *(Chapter 1)*

When predictor variables recorded at the time of abuse were tested against Index children's outcomes there were no very strong relationships. There was some evidence that combined neglect and abuse, and widespread family violence, might be associated with poorer outcomes. In general, circumstances existing at the time of abuse were not useful predictors of outcomes ten years later, probably because so many changes had since occurred in the lives of the Index children. *(Chapter 2)*

At a minimum estimate, 20% had suffered physical abuse (rarely causing any serious injury) since registration and 5% had suffered sexual abuse. Altogether 24% had suffered one or other or both forms of subsequent abuse. No relationship could be found between subsequent abuse and children's overall outcomes. Other life events, such as changes in carers, schools or address also had no clear relationship with outcomes. The incidence of subsequent abuse and life events was concentrated in the two or three years after registration. By the time of follow-up most children's lives had become more settled. *(Chapter 3)*

Parenting styles at the time of follow-up were strongly related to outcomes in both Index and Comparison groups. When parents used critical, punitive styles and physical punishment children had more behaviour problems, higher depression scores and more friendship problems. Children who saw their parents as strict and who described warmly positive relationships with them had fewer behaviour problems and better cognitive performance. Index children were more often exposed to punitive parenting styles and physical punishment. Their parents were more burdened with personal problems and less satisfied with social support. There was more violence between the adult partners in the Index families. *(Chapter 4)*

Interviews with Index and Comparison children supported the view that children were likely to do less well if they were exposed to inconsistent discipline that included physical punishment and if they saw parents as unreliable and showing little warmth and affection. *(Chapter 5)*

Over three-quarters of the Index children had experienced a loss of or change in parent figures by the time of follow-up. This instability was partly caused by protective action (by parents themselves as well as officials) to separate child from abuser, especially following any repetition. Forty-two children were in more or less permanent substitute care – 17% of these were fostered with relatives; 38% fostered with non-relatives; 43% adopted; and only one in residential care. The children in substitute care at follow-up did not differ greatly from the remainder on baseline characteristics, but their families had been poorer at the time of registration and parental neglect had more often been recorded. *(Chapter 6)*

Adopted children had been in their families for at least 7 years, having mostly been placed before the age of 3. Foster children had joined their families at older ages on average. The whole 'separated' group had generally moved from the most disadvantaged circumstances at the time of abuse to the most privileged at the time of follow-up. Adoption or foster care had brought major material advantage. *(Chapter 6)*

The 'separated' group as a whole scored better on measures of physical growth and vocabulary. This was most likely due to their higher social class. 'Separated' children were rated by teachers as showing more prosocial behaviour, but they had as many behaviour problems at home and school and adopted children had higher depression scores. *(Chapter 6)*

No clear relationships could be found between age at placement and children's outcomes. *(Chapter 6)*

There was a consistent trend for adopted children to show more behaviour problems, more friendship problems and more depression compared with children in foster care. A possible explanatory factor was the foster carers' greater success in avoiding punitive parenting styles and physical punishment. *(Chapter 6)*

The pattern of services provided by the key agency was examined separately for children in substitute care and those with natural parents. There was some evidence that more intensive and prolonged social work contact had some benefits for children who remained with their own parents, and that for them packages of service that included psychiatric treatment for a parent, support from a voluntary agency or therapeutic attendance at a family centre were beneficial. *(Chapter 7)*

Introduction

This report describes a nine to ten year follow-up study of pre-school children placed on child protection registers. The great majority of them had been physically harmed. Children aged one to four are the age-group most likely to be placed on registers in England, with a rate of 4.6 per thousand in 1992, and the commonest specific reason for registration is physical abuse, accounting for 26% of cases in 1992 (Department of Health, 1993). The numbers of children identified as physically harmed by their parents or caregivers have been rising since figures were first recorded – at first by the National Society for the Prevention of Cruelty to Children (NSPCC) and later by the Department of Health. Child protection takes priority over more general preventive work with families in local authority social services departments and the consequences of mistakes are grave indeed. Yet there is surprisingly little large-scale research in Britain which can provide evidence on what actually happens to children who have been registered as in need of protection and who have received different kinds of service.

Researchers are challenged by the methodological problems of carrying out good research on this topic, which cause a degree of uncertainty still to exist over the longer-term consequences of physical maltreatment. Do children suffer long-term, serious damage as a consequence of physical abuse? Or are many of the alleged consequences really due to growing up in deprived social circumstances? We know that poverty produces major consequences for health and even expectation of life, as well as for individual opportunity and chances of success (Bradshaw, 1990). The methodological issues we had in the forefront of our minds when designing the study were the need to be more specific about the circumstance in which physical injury took place, so that more homogenous groups could be defined; the need for adequate comparison groups of children who had not been physically maltreated; the need to use measures of outcome that had some theoretical justification, were appropriate to the children's ages and that could be replicated.

The starting-point of the research was our desire to study the effects of protective intervention on the well-being of particular children deemed to be at risk. We reasoned that while the major purpose of the child protection system should be to safeguard children from death or serious injury and sexual harm, under the Children Act 1989 the services also have a duty to promote the welfare of children in need. This in turn means that services should promote the chances of children developing normally and achieving their full potential. Thus an important test of the child protection system's success would be the extent to which children exposed to its intervention, and under the protection of a key agency, did in fact develop normally. Others have examined the longer-term consequences of child maltreatment. Our approach was different in that we did not start from a theoretical interest or expertise in child development. Our purpose was much more limited. As social work researchers, we wished to provide information that would be useful to social workers and other professionals charged with the responsibility for taking action intended to safeguard children from significant harm.

Workers in the child protection system repeatedly have to take decisions (which may radically affect the lives of children and parents) in conditions of great uncertainty. We hoped that studying the consequences that have followed from such decisions could provide information to help workers who have to weigh up the balance of probabilities and decide what action to take in particular cases. This information could also be useful to policy makers who have to make decisions about the allocation of resources; and to parents themselves when decisions are being taken about treatment or intervention plans.

It is impossible, for ethical reasons, to study effectiveness of services through experiments in which maltreated children are randomly allocated to different conditions. Longitudinal studies, which can take advantage of naturally occurring variations in amount and type of intervention, are therefore the best way of obtaining evidence on the effects of different types of service. However, because serious maltreatment is a comparatively rare event, prospective longitudinal research on children in the general population would be prohibitively expensive – a sample size of 10 000 might be necessary in order to find 50 subjects. For reasons of feasibility and expense, we chose a 'high risk' sample (Rutter & Garmezy, 1983), and a retrospective type of follow-up design.

Aims of study

The study took a sample of children who had been placed on child protection registers when they were under five years old as a result of physical ill-treatment. These children (the Index sample) were studied again approximately ten years later, in order to assess:

- physical growth
- cognitive ability and school achievement
- emotional and behaviour problems
- relationships with peers.

The yardstick of 'normal' development was not a measure of 'ideal' development. Normal development was defined by the performance of children of the same age and sex who lived nearby and attended the same schools – who, in short were expected to resemble the Index sample closely, except that they had never been notified to the child protection system. For the purposes of the study, 'normal' was to be defined by the performance of this Comparison sample.

The services provided to the Index sample at the time of registration and during the follow-up period were documented through the records of the key agency.

Our intention was to throw light on the following issues:

1. What were the longer term consequences of ill-treatment? Were there any major differences in development between the Index children, who had been ill-treated in early life, and the Comparison children, who had not come into contact with the child protection system? Did any differences hold when socio-economic status was controlled?

2. Did the circumstances in which children were injured – the extent of injury, the context of family problems etc – make any difference to longer-term development or to the chance of repetition of abuse? Were there specific risk factors that existed at the time of abuse and 'predicted' poor outcome nine to ten years later?[1]

3. What life events had the Index children experienced during the follow-up period? Did those children who experienced more turbulence and life changes have any worse outcomes?

4. What were the family relationships of the Index children some ten years after ill-treatment? Did they experience different styles of parenting from the Comparison children? Did current family relationships influence their performance on the measures of development?

5. What services had been provided by the key agency? What was the quality of services, in terms of amount and range, continuity, evidence of planning?

6. Did different kinds of service provision appear to be associated with different outcomes? In particular, did children removed from their parents and placed in new families show any better outcomes? Did placement in secure, permanent new families through adoption compensate for the early experiences of physical harm?

The Report is organised in three sections. For the reader's convenience we have departed from the usual convention and placed the description of our findings at the beginning in Part 1. Chapter 1 describes the developmental

---

[1] The word 'outcome' is used throughout as a summary term for the children's status on measures of development at the time of follow-up. 'Outcome' is not meant to imply an effect or result of treatment.

outcomes of the formerly abused and comparison children. Chapter 2 attempts to identify 'predictors' of outcome from the circumstances surrounding the original abuse. Chapter 3 describes the life events to which the Index children were exposed in the period following abuse. Chapter 4 compares the family relationships of the Index and Comparison children; and Part 1 ends with a comparison of their own views of their worlds, derived from their own words. Part 2 describes the protective and supportive services that were supplied to the Index children and examines the relationships with outcome measures. Chapter 6 in this Part looks at the effects of placement in permanent adoptive homes or long-stay foster care. Part 3, written by Bernard Gallagher, sets the study in a broader context with a comprehensive review of the literature (chapter 8); and gives a full description of the methodology (chapter 9). The results are evaluated in the Conclusions – chapter 10.

PART ONE

Consequences of Physical Maltreatment

Chapter 1

The development of children nine to ten years after physical abuse

Interest in the longer-term consequences of physical abuse upon children's development began soon after the 'rediscovery' of physical cruelty to children in the early 1960s. Although Kempe and colleagues (1962) had coined the term *battered child syndrome*, with its evocation of horrifying physical injuries, it probably became clear at an early stage that most children who suffered non-accidental injury were not badly hurt. Doctors were anxious to identify more subtly damaging consequences of the maltreatment they observed and follow-up studies were undertaken. Table 1.i summarises results from controlled follow-up or longitudinal studies of physically abused children. There is disagreement over whether physical abuse produces effects upon children over and above the effects on them of growing up in poverty. Elmer (1977), for instance, compared 17 physically abused children with a matched group of children injured in accidents one year and eight to nine years after their original admission to hospital. She found few differences between them and another matched group hospitalised for non-traumatic reasons. As she put it,

> It was impossible to avoid the conclusion that abuse as one method of deviant child care did not appear to make a significant difference. <The factor underlying the high rate of pathology observed in all groups> was membership of the majority in the lower social classes, which connotes poverty and all its well-known companions: poor education, menial jobs, inadequate housing, under-nutrition, poor health and environmental violence.

However, more recent research has generally found that physical abuse does have damaging longer-term consequences over and above the effects of growing up in poverty. Egeland and colleagues, in a prospective study of children born to disadvantaged mothers, compared physically abused children with children receiving good care. By the age of two the abused group were behind in development and were showing difficult behaviour with their mothers. By the age of six there were significant differences in school attainment and behaviour, with twice as many of the formerly abused being in the least competent cluster (Erickson et al., 1989). Oates (1984) found significant differences between 39 formerly abused children and a matched comparison group in IQ, behaviour and personality. Widom (1989) in a large cohort study found that abused and neglected children were more likely subsequently to be arrested for juvenile delinquency and adult crime.

It has been suggested that children suffering abuse in early life are likely to show such long-lasting consequences because of the effects on early attachment to parent figures. This disturbance in early relationships may have pervasive effects on children's socio-emotional development, best described as organisational: the balance between "security-promoting operations" and "competence-promoting operations" is distorted, leading to difficulties in adapting to new environments, learning and making friends (Aber et al., 1989).

The question whether physical abuse of itself causes significant harm to children's development is of more than academic importance. If children experience neither serious physical damage (as few of them do) nor long-term socio-emotional consequences then there is less reason to give such high priority to child protection. If poverty and disadvantage are the over-riding influences on child development then services for children and families should logically be organised to compensate as far as possible for their effects. This would entail giving more priority to services which increase resources in impoverished neighbourhoods and less priority to detection and treatment of maltreatment in individual cases. However a problem in drawing clear conclusions from the existing literature is the small size of the samples, their lack of homogeneity, the questionable representativeness of hospital-based samples, the problem of finding appropriate comparison groups and the difficulties of generalising from different cultures (see Part 3 for fuller discussion).

Aim of chapter

This chapter will examine the effects of physical abuse before the age of five (over and above the effects of social status) upon children's physical growth, behaviour, friendships and school performance nine to ten years later. Our initial hypothesis was that formerly abused children would have worse outcomes in all these aspects of development than similar children who had not been abused, when socio-economic status was controlled.

Methods

A full account of the methods is contained in Part 3. For the reader's convenience a summary is included here.

Abused and comparison groups

The total sample consisted of 170 children – all those who, before the age of five, had been placed on registers operated by the NSPCC during one year. The NSPCC's criteria for entry to the register were:

Table 1.i **Physical abuse: follow-up studies**

Author	Sample	Comparison	Yrs	Trace	Age	Ses	Findings
Elmer (1977)	24 in hosp	76 acc. trauma	1	?	1–2	Yes	No diffs: height, weight, development, behaviour. Abused more accidents and health problems.
ibid	17	17 acc. trauma 25 untraum. hosp.	8	71%	8–9	Yes	No diffs in language, impulsivity, aggression, empathy, self-concept. Abused more neurological probs. (?from birth). No different in school ability but high certainty abused worse on teacher ratings of frustration tolerance and interest in school. Abu in substitute homes fared worse.
Friedman & Morse (1974)	22 abused & neglected in hosp.	19 acc. trauma	5	75%	5–10	No	Abused had more re-injuries.
Lynch & Roberts (1982)	39 in IP treatment	41 unharmed sibs	4	93%	?4–5	Yes	Sig. pre-abuse diffs: more pre-term, neo-natal illness, neurol. impairment & devel. delay. At follow-up no sig. diffs in devel., IQ, behaviour (Rutter A & Bristol SAG). Abused & sibs worse than pop. Sibs born after abuse best outcome.
Oates (1986)	39 ? source	Matched unharmed	5.5	36%	8.9	Yes	Abused lower IQ, reading, self-esteem. Fewer friends. More behav. probs (Rutter A & B). Parents more isolated. Had high school expectations but provided less supervision and direction.
Calam & Franchi (1987)	38 on register	76 classmates	5	72%	5–11	No	No different in school attainment. Abused, esp boys, had worse school adjustment (over-reaction on BSAG). Type of injury and repetition had no effect on outcome. Abused with sg parents worse as were abused who experienced short periods of care.

Study	Abused	Comparison	YRS	TRACE	AGE	SES	Findings
Erickson et al (1989)	32 maltreated from 267 disad. mothers	33 good care mothers	<1	NA	<1	?	No differences.
			18/12		18/12	?	Abused more anxious attachments.
ibid	24 physically abused	85 good care	2	?	2	?	Abused lower developmental scores. More angry behaviour with mothers. More distractible, less confident on task. Non-compliant, avoided mothers on task.
ibid	16 physically abused	65 unharmed	6	66% 76%	6	?	Abused more impulsive, negativistic, dependent on task. Lower cognitive scores. Teachers rated more inattentive, unpopular, aggressive & overactive. 44% v 21% referred for special help. 56% v 27% in least competent cluster. Environmental predictors: maternal stability, mood, IQ. Quality of home. Life events.
Widom (1989)	908 abused & neg. from court records	667 matched from birth & school records	20	NA	11–31	Yes	Maltreated had more arrests for juvenile & adult crimes & more violent criminality.

YRS: Length of follow-up period
TRACE: % of original cases successfully followed-up
AGE: Mean age at follow-up
SES: Control for socio-economic status

All physically injured children under the age of 17 years where the nature of the injury is not consistent with the account of how it occurred or where there is definite knowledge, or a reasonable suspicion , that the injury was inflicted (or knowingly not prevented) by any person having custody, charge or care of the child. This includes children to whom it is suspected poisonous substances have been administered. Diagnosis of child abuse will normally require both medical examination of the child and social assessment.

For each formerly abused (Index) child three Comparison children were identified of the same gender, age, school and area of residence, the majority through the index system of the school medical service but a few through direct approach to schools. Their names were checked against local records and those who had been notified to the register or subject to a legal order were excluded.

At follow-up nine to ten years after the Index children were placed on the register 165 out of 170 were traced to an address in Britain; three had emigrated; one had died; only one was not traced. Once traced, caregivers were sent an introductory letter explaining the purpose of the research as being to study the development of a large group of children, some of whom had experienced problems in early childhood, and asking permission for a research interviewer to visit. Once the Index child and his or her main caregiver had been interviewed the same introductory letter was sent to the Comparison group family whose child was nearest in birthdate, who was approached in the same way. The next Comparison child was substituted in case of a refusal.

Measures of children's development

Age-appropriate indicators covering different developmental capacities were chosen as follows.

Growth

Measurement of height, weight and head circumference

Behaviour

(i) At home: Rutter A questionnaire (Rutter et al., 1970)
(ii) At school: Rutter B questionnaire (Rutter et al., 1970)
              Prosocial questionnaire (Weir & Duveen, 1981)

Emotions

Child's self-reported fears (Ollendick, 1983)
Self-reported depression (Birleson et al., 1981)

Problems with peers

Items from interview with child:

Would like more friends
Needs friends quite a bit
Is often bullied
Bullies others
Would like to spend more time with kids his/her age

Cognitive ability
Raven's Progressive Matrices (Raven et al., 1976)
British Ability Scales (Elliott et al., 1983)
British Picture Vocabulary Scale (Dunn et al., 1982)

The interviews were carried out by four experienced women interviewers after preliminary training. They were blind to the study's purpose and did not know whether children were in Index or Comparison groups. They obtained written consent from caregivers and separately from children. Parents and children were paid small sums for their time. The interviews normally took place in the child's home and wherever possible children were seen alone.

Physical measurements were carried out by trained nurses. Cognitive testing was done by specially trained teachers who visited the children by arrangement at school or sometimes at home.

Response rate

144 out of 170 Index children and caregivers agreed to take part – 85% of the total sample or 87% of the families actually approached (figure 1). The missing cases were no different in age, but more of them were girls (69% compared to 44% in the total sample). The missing cases appeared otherwise to be a mixed group, including some quite settled children as well as a few in serious difficulties. The 87 Index boys who took part had a mean age at the time of follow-up of 11.68 (Comparison boys 11.62). The 57 Index girls had a mean age of 11.33 (Comparison girls 11.31).

In considering how well the children fared in the years after being placed on the child protection register we decided, first to focus on their performance over a wide range of indicators; and second, to put this performance in the context of the achievements of other children, of the same age-group and sex, who attended the same schools and lived in the same local areas. We recognised that these Comparison children would not be a representative sample of the normal child population, in that they would be weighted towards lower socio-economic status, and lower academic ability. They were chosen as a group of children who would be of similar social status to the Index sample but who differed in never having been referred to a child protection register.

Results

We will first examine how similar the Index and Comparison children in fact proved to be.

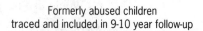
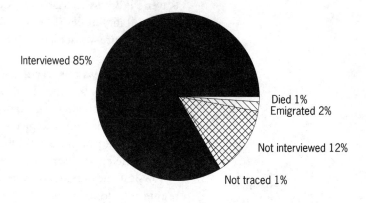

Formerly abused children
traced and included in 9-10 year follow-up

N = 170 children

Figure 1   Children included in follow-up

Social background of Index and Comparison children

Family structure

There were marked differences in household composition (though not in household size). 35% of Index children were in lone-parent households (compared with 23% of Comparison children). Only 26% of the Index were living with two adults, both of whom were the joint parents of all the children in the household (compared with 59%). The Index children were more often in reconstituted families, with a step-parent (23% v 16%). They were more likely to be with adults neither of whom was a natural nor an adopted parent (16% v 2%).

Race

There were no significant differences in ethnic background between the Index and Comparison children, although rather fewer were described by their parents as 'white' (82% v 90%), and rather more as 'mixed parentage' (11% v 5%). Approximately equal numbers were described as 'black' (5% v 3%) and 'Asian' (both 2%).

Social class

There were no significant differences in the current social class of the Index and Comparison children, as measured by the present or last occupation of the head of household. Figure 2 shows the social class distribution. There were no significant differences, illustrating the success of combining school and area of residence in the process of selecting the Comparison children. However, there would undoubtedly have been a different class distribution if all the Index children had remained with their original parents. Those in adoptive households had almost invariably improved their social class position.

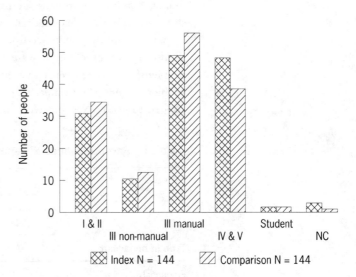

Figure 2   Social class of head of household

Poverty and housing

However, the social class classification was problematic, since more Index families were headed by lone, usually female parents who had often not worked for many years. In addition to assigned social class an Index of Disadvantage was constructed for each child, using absence of a wage-earner, lack of secure housing, large number of children, overcrowding and lack of consumer goods (Gibbons et al., 1990). In spite of their similarity in social class status, the Index children were living in households with more indicators of poverty and bad housing (mean 1.3 v 0.9 F6.9 sig. .008). Thus in interpreting differences in outcome it was necessary to take social disadvantage as well as assigned social class into account.

Index children's households were more mobile: 15% had lived at their present address for less than a year (compared with 8%). They had moved house on average 1.2 times in the last 5 years (0.4 times).

In summary, although there were no significant differences between Index and Comparison children in social class or racial background, there were important differences in household composition, poverty and mobility. Some of these changes were no doubt due to the process of reconstituting households that often followed – sooner or later – the official recognition of abuse.

Children's behaviour at home

The parent questionnaire contained 31 items concerned with the child's health, habits and behaviour. Sub-scores concerned emotional disorder (5 items), conduct disorder (5 items), and over-activity (3 items). Table 1.ii shows the results. Index children had more emotional difficulties (as observed by parents) but the difference from Comparison children was not statistically significant. Index children were significantly more likely to have conduct problems and to be over-active. Index children had significantly raised total problem scores. The differences between Index and Comparison children applied to both sexes, but were more marked for girls.

Table 1.ii **Parents' ratings of behaviour: Index and Comparison children**

	Boys		Girls	
	Index (91)	Comparison (91)	Index (53)	Comparison (53)
Type of behaviour	Mean scores			
Emotional	2.1	1.9	2.1	1.8
Conduct	2.5	1.6**	2.3	1.0**
Over-activity	2.2	1.7*	1.7	0.8*
Total behaviour	13.9	11.1*	13.9	8.8**

Oneway analysis of variance:
* Difference likely to occur by chance less than 5 in 100
** Difference likely to occur by chance less than 1 in 100

Teacher ratings of behaviour

Class teachers answered two different questionnaires about children's behaviour at school. The Rutter B Scale consisted of 26 brief statements about the child's behaviour scored (as was the parent scale) 2 for 'certainly applies', 1 'applies somewhat' and 0 'does not apply'. Four of the items made up a Neurotic sub-score and 6 items made up an Antisocial subscore. The

Prosocial Scale (Weir & Duveen, 1981) consisted of 20 statements concerned with the child's positive behaviour at school, scored 2 for 'certainly applies', 1 for 'applies somewhat' and 0 for 'rarely applies'. The results are illustrated in table 1.iii. On the teacher ratings the Index boys (but not the girls) scored higher on the Neurotic sub-score as well as the Antisocial sub-score. Teachers rated Index girls markedly higher on the Antisocial subscale. The difference in total Rutter score was greater for boys than for girls. The Prosocial score, however, did not discriminate between Index and Comparison boys, while there were marked differences between girls.

Table 1.iii **Teachers' ratings of behaviour: Index and Comparison children**

	Boys		Girls	
	Index (88)	**Comparison (87)**	**Index (49)**	**Comparison (49)**
Type of behaviour	**Mean scores**			
Neurotic	2.1	1.3**	1.6	1.7
Antisocial	2.8	1.7*	2.0	0.5**
Total Rutter Scale	12.1	7.7**	8.5	5.0*
Prosocial Scale	17.8	19.1	22.5	27.7**

Missing data on 7 Index and 8 Comparison cases
* Difference likely to occur by chance less than 5 in 100
** Difference likely to occur by chance less than 1 in 100

When the Rutter Scale was validated on general population and clinic samples, 11% of boys and 3.5% of girls in the population obtained a score of 9 or more. In the present study, 61% of Index (and 39% of Comparison) boys obtained this score; as did 43% of Index (and 20% of Comparison) girls. Thus the Comparison children in the present study were considerably more disturbed than the validating population sample.

It is likely that if the Index children in the present study had been compared with randomly selected children in the population, the differences found between the groups would have been even greater. However, it should be noted that the Index children were not showing the same degree of disturbance as did the original clinic samples, where 80% of boys and 60% of girls scored above the cut-off.

Teacher and parent ratings of children's behaviour were moderately positively correlated ($r=0.45$ $p<.001$).

A statistician (Dr Gordon) carried out reliability analysis of the three questionnaires. Coefficient Alpha (Cronbach, 1951) for the Prosocial scale was .934; for Rutter B (teacher ratings) it was .892; and for Rutter A (parent ratings) it was .602. Nunnally (1978) states that reliabilities of .70 or more are acceptable and that it is wasteful to seek to increase reliabilities beyond .80. Thus both the Prosocial and Rutter B teacher questionnaires were highly reliable in the present study but the Rutter A parent questionnaire was less so.

Behavioural items

The items which significantly differentiated the Index from the Comparison group make up a sad picture of some children, who were perceived as unpopular, solitary, often miserable, unable to keep still, disobedient, aggressive and destructive. Table 1.iv summarises the items.

Table 1.iv **Behaviour items discriminating between Index and Comparison children**

Item	Parent	Teacher
Stealing	✓	
Squirmy, fidgety	✓	✓
Very restless		✓
Not much liked	✓	✓
Solitary	✓	
Often disobedient	✓	✓
Cannot settle for more than a few minutes	✓	✓
Often tells lies	✓	✓
Often destroys property		✓
Frequently fights		✓
Irritable, touchy		✓
Often miserable		✓
Resentful/aggressive if corrected		✓

Relationships with peers

An index was constructed from children's answers to five interview questions about their friendships (see page 10). The possible range of peer problems was thus from 0 to 5. Index children had significantly more difficulties with peers than did Comparison children. This was true of boys and girls, but girls showed the greatest difference (table 1.v)

Children's fears and depression

At interview, the children were invited to answer a questionnaire which contained simple statements about feelings of misery and depression (Birleson Questionnaire). Girls tended towards expressing more feelings of depression than boys but there were no differences between the Index and Comparison groups. The children also completed a checklist of things that made them afraid (Ollendick Questionnaire). There was a trend for Index girls to report more fears than Comparison girls but no significant difference between the samples (table 1.vi).

Table 1.v **Problems with peers**

	Boys		**Girls**	
	Mean problems			
Index	1.83	sd 1.3	1.85	sd 1.3
Comparison	1.39	sd 1.2	1.19	sd 1.0
	F=5.16	sig. .024	F=9.0	sig. .003

Missing data on 2 Index boys and girls and 3 Comparison boys

Table 1.vi **Fears and depression: Index and Comparison children**

	Boys		**Girls**	
	Index (85)	**Comparison (87)**	**Index (50)**	**Comparison (48)**
Scale	**Means**			
Fears Scale	26.05	24.35	31.65	27.60
Depression Scale	8.99	8.48	9.9	9.36

Missing data on 9 Index and 9 Comparison cases

Cognitive performance

The children were in a variety of different types of school in different parts of the country. Eleven of the Index children (7%) were currently at special schools; another seven (5%) had been given statements of special needs but were still in mainstream schools; and six more were attending special classes, although they had not been 'statemented'. Thus a high proportion were showing serious academic problems. The Comparison children of course attended the same schools by virtue of the matching procedure.

The mean age of boys at testing was 11.68 (Index) and 11.61 (Comparison). For girls the mean age was 11.32 (11.3). The educational tests are more fully described in Part 3. Results are presented in this book in summary form only.

1. Raven's progressive matrices

This test was used as a measure of abstract reasoning capacity that is also quite enjoyable for children to take. Table 1.vii shows the percentile distribution of Index and Comparison children. The Index children were more concentrated in the lower percentile ranges, but the differences were not statistically significant. In making the comparison, it must be remembered that the children were drawn from the same school classes – thus if a member of the Index sample was in a special school, so would be the corresponding Comparison child.

2. Skills of language and number

The British Picture Vocabulary Scale was used as a measure of receptive vocabulary. The British Ability Scales were used to test verbal ability (Similarities Test), basic number skills and word reading. Table 1.viii shows

Table 1.vii **Distribution of Index and Comparison children on percentile ranges of Raven's progressive matrices**

	Boys		Girls	
	Index (87)	Comparison (86)	Index (51)	Comparison (50)
Percentile range	per cent			
95 & over 'superior'	1	2	–	4
75–94 'above average'	9	17	20	20
26–74 'average'	51	56	39	50
6–25 'below average'	28	19	27	22
5 & below 'impaired'	11	6	14	4
All	100	100	100	100

Missing data on 6 Index and 8 Comparison cases

Table 1.viii **Performance on tests of language and number skills**

	Boys		Girls	
	Index (87)	Comparison (86)	Index (51)	Comparison (50)
Test	**Mean score**			
BPVS	90.7	96.1	89.9	93.6
BAS Similarities	45.4	48.5	45.4	47.5
BAS Basic number	38.8	41.8	41.0	44.3
BAS Word Reading	43.9	46.4	46.6	47.3

Missing data on 6 Index and 8 Comparison cases

the standardised mean scores on these tests. (The BPVS has a standardised mean of 100, and the British Ability Scales one of 50). The Comparison boys were performing significantly better than the Index boys on all except the Word Reading Test. The Comparison girls performed significantly better on the test of Basic Number. The differences, however, were not particularly striking, and the performance of both groups of children was depressed in comparison with national norms.

Physical development

It has been suggested that a possible long-term effect of physical abuse might be to limit children's physical growth. In order to test this hypothesis, nurses were employed to weigh and measure the children under controlled conditions at school.

Table 1.ix **Physical measurements of Index and Comparison children**

	Boys		Girls	
	Index (88)	Comparison (85)	Index (50)	Comparison (48)
Measure	**Means**			
Height (metres)	1.44	1.45	1.43	1.43
Weight (kg)	37.5	38.2	37.9	39.7
Head circumference (cm)	53.1	53.1	52.8	53.1

Missing data on 6 Index and 11 Comparison cases

In table 1.ix the results of these measurements are summarised. It can be seen that there were few differences in the growth rate of Index and Comparison children.

In summary, the formerly abused children as a group had significantly more behaviour problems at home and at school and reported more difficulties with peers than the Comparison group of children who had not suffered abuse. They also scored worse on some tests of attainment. However, they were no different in height and weight, nor on self-reported fears and depression.

Best discriminators

Many of the separate outcome measures were highly inter-correlated with each other. The next step was to find the combination of measures that best discriminated between the Index and Comparison groups ie that best characterised the longer-term consequences of the early physical abuse suffered by the former. Using stepwise discriminant analysis Dr Gordon selected five variables that best discriminated the groups: the Parents' behaviour rating (Rutter A); Problems with Peers; British Ability Scale measuring verbal ability; Teachers' behaviour ratings (Rutter B); and the Rutter A Emotions subscale. This latter is likely to be merely a statistical artefact, just happening to combine with the other four variables to produce the best discrimination.

The likelihood of the discrimination between Index and Comparison children being due to chance was less than 1 in 10 000. However, this overstates the importance of the difference between the two groups. Using canonical correlation, the five variables in combination were found to explain only 15.2% of the variance. The percentage of cases correctly classified shows how well the discriminant function predicted the actual membership of the two groups. In this case the discriminant analysis correctly classified 68% of cases – 36% better than random. After cross-validation the proportion correctly classified fell very little – 33% better than random. Thus the analysis showed that there were real differences in developmental capacities between schoolchildren who had experienced physical abuse in early life and similar children who had not. However, the differences were not very large and there was considerable overlap between the two groups, as figure 3 demonstrates.

Outcome profiles

There was, therefore a wide range of developmental outcomes in both Index and Comparison groups. So far we have examined these outcomes along a range of dimensions. In addition to looking at performance and behaviour along these separate dimensions, we also wanted to find a way of combining the data so that for each child there was an 'outcome profile'. By

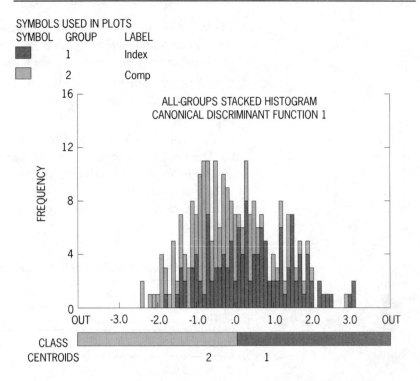

SYMBOLS USED IN PLOTS
SYMBOL   GROUP   LABEL
           1   Index
           2   Comp

** Above is a histogram of the discriminant function values of all 230 cases.
The Discriminant Analysis Function can be used to produce a rule that best discriminates between the two groups (Index and Comparison children) based on the five selected variables. The actual values of the discriminant function for each case can then be compared with the predicted values. If the Discriminant analysis has worked perfectly then all Index Children will be in the right half of the Histogram and all the comparison children on the left. There are considerable number of cases in the wrong halves of the histogram which shows that the discriminant rule is not correct for these cases.

Figure 3   Distribution of Index and Comparison children on outcome measures

this means we hoped at least to be able to identify a group of children who were doing particularly badly over a range of outcome measures, and a group who were doing particularly well. It was already clear that these groups would not divide along the lines of our two samples, but that some of the formerly abused were doing unusually well, while some of the Comparison children were doing badly.

An independent statistician, who at this stage was blind to other information about the children, derived four 'outcome factors', using all the measures except those of physical growth. The factors summarised parents' perceptions of children's behaviour at home; teachers' ratings of behaviour at school; educational performance; and children's self-reported fears and miseries. These factor scores were then used to group the children into three outcome clusters (See Appendix A).

Cluster 1 contains children whose outcome was very poor. They had above average parent and teacher ratings of behaviour problems, a low educational performance score and above average fears/depression scores.

Cluster 2 on the other hand contains children with a good overall outcome – low parent and teacher ratings of behaviour problems, high educational performance and low fear/depression.

Cluster 3 appears to be an intermediate group, with low school performance but fewer behaviour problems and average fears/depression.

The Index children, as expected, were significantly over-represented in the cluster identified with poor outcome, and under-represented in the 'good outcome' cluster. Similar proportions were in the 'low performance' cluster (Table 1.x).

Table 1.x   **Outcome profiles of Index and Comparison children**

Cluster	Index		Comparison	
	N	**%**	**N**	**%**
Cluster 1: Poor outcome	54	42	25	19
Cluster 2: Good outcome	28	22	61	48
Cluster 3: Low performance	47	36	42	33
All	129	100	128	100

Chi square 23.15 df2 sig. .0000
Some data missing on 15 Index and 16 Comparison cases

It was noteworthy, then, that about a fifth of the Index children seemed to have overcome the problems of their early life, to the extent that they were now relatively high achievers, without apparent behaviour or emotional problems. Conversely, almost a fifth of the Comparison children, who had not been victims of physical abuse, were displaying serious behavioural and academic problems.

Effects of socio-economic status

In the total population of children in the study, higher social class was associated with significantly better performance on the cognitive tests. (Social class however had no significant association with the behavioural ratings). Social class affected cognitive performance differently in the Index and Comparison groups. The educational performance factor (summarising scores on the cognitive tests) showed a linear decline in the Comparison group – above average in children from managerial and professional backgrounds to below average in children from unskilled or semi-skilled manual backgrounds. The picture was different in the Index group. Children from professional or managerial backgrounds did not perform so well and children in the lowest social class group did not perform so badly. In terms of cognitive performance, the biggest discrepancy between Index and Comparison children was found in social classes one and two, at the top, while Comparison children in social classes four and five were actually performing slightly worse than Index children (Table 1.xi). The explanation may be found in the fact that a high proportion of the Index children in social classes one and two were there as a result of adoption or foster care, while this was not true of the Comparison children.

Table 1.xi **Social class and cognitive performance**

Social class	Index	Comparison	Sig.
	Cognitive performance factor		
1 & 2	0.08	3.49	.002
3 non-manual	0.99	0.45	NS
3 manual	−1.76	0.21	.006
4 & 5	−0.87	−0.95	NS

We have shown that Index and Comparison groups did not differ in social class distribution, but that Index children were living in significantly more socially disadvantaged circumstances. Levels of disadvantage were strongly associated with outcome measures in the total population of children. The greater the disadvantage the worse the behavioural ratings, the more problems with peers and the worse the performance on the cognitive tests. Did the differences between Index and Comparison children persist when levels of disadvantage were controlled? Or did the more impoverished circumstances of the Index group account for their poorer overall outcomes?

Multivariate analysis of variance was undertaken for each outcome measure from the set of best discriminators, controlling for child's age and gender, social class, disadvantage and household type. Four measures (parents' and teachers' ratings of behaviour, problems with peers and verbal reasoning ability) continued to discriminate between Index and Comparison children when these social background factors were controlled (table 1.xii).

We conclude, therefore, that there were real differences between the children who had suffered early abuse and those who had not, differences which could not be explained by age, gender, social class or disadvantage.

However, within each group there was a wide spread of performance, with approaching a quarter of formerly abused children showing excellent all-round results.

Table 1.xii **Index and Comparison group differences after controlling for social background**

Outcome variable	F	Sig.
Rutter A Score	16.7	.000
Rutter B Score	13.8	.000
Peer problems	13.8	.000
British Ability Scale	7.9	.005

Chapter 2

The abuse and its context

In the previous chapter we saw that although, on average, formerly abused children had more behavioural problems and relationship difficulties and poorer attainment on some tests than similar children who had not suffered abuse, yet there was a wide range of outcomes in the group. Did the circumstances in which the original abuse occurred explain any of the differences in outcome within the Index group?

To recapitulate, children entered the study if, in 1981 when they were aged under 5, they had been placed on child protection registers maintained by the NSPCC in two areas (City and County). One of the reasons for choosing these registers as the source of the sample was that the NSPCC at that time used standard methods of recording details of children and their families who were placed on the registers it operated. After the case conference, details of the injury and the children's social circumstances were entered onto standard NSPCC forms by NSPCC register staff. These records were used in the NSPCC's ongoing, centrally managed research programme (Creighton, 1985). Thus we were able to have access to information which had been recorded in a systematic way at the time of the original abuse, and did not have to rely on memories of what had occurred.

Aim of chapter

This chapter will describe the circumstances in which the abuse occurred nine to ten years previously and whether it was possible to identify circumstances at the time of abuse that 'predicted' children's outcomes at the time of the follow-up.

Severity of injury

The great majority (86%) had been physically injured. The remainder were considered by the case conference in 1981 to be at serious risk of injury (including a few cases of failure to thrive).

The NSPCC employed a standard definition of severity, as follows:

'Fatal':   All cases resulting in death

'Serious':   Fractures, head injuries, internal injuries, severe burns, ingestion of toxic substances

'Moderate': Soft tissue injuries of superficial nature.

Of the 170 cases in the sample, 89% of those with any injury fell into the 'moderate' category, as classified by the NSPCC. We broke this category down further by introducing a new class of 'slight' injuries. These were soft-tissue injuries which affected only one body part – such as a slap on the arm. 74 children (50% of those injured) received 'slight' injuries. Table 2.i illustrates the means used to inflict injury in relation to the severity of injury caused. Shaking was particularly likely to cause serious injury in these young children.

Table 2.i **Severity and method of injury**

Method	N	Serious %	Moderate %	Slight %
Burning	11	24	8	4
Cutting	1	0	2	0
Hit/object	21	9	23	15
Pull/shake	29	52	15	17
Drop/throw	7	5	5	6
Hit/hand	52	5	44	49
Other	8	5	3	9
All	129	21	39	69

23 cases uninjured. 18 cases method NK

In summary then, only 16% of the children sustained serious physical injury in 1981 – a fairly typical proportion. NSPCC figures for all its registers (1977–1981) show that 20% were seriously injured, but a Scottish study found that in a sample of under-fives registered in 1982–3, less than 10% had sustained serious injury (Gough et al., 1987). The commonest method of inflicting injury was a slap with the hand. We might expect that, if physical abuse produces specific longer-term consequences, the children who received some injury would have worse outcomes than those who were never injured; and those with more severe injuries might fare worse.

Co-existence of neglect

In 18% of cases neglect definitely, and in 15% probably, co-existed with injury. In cases of injury alone, the perpetrator was more likely to be male, there was more often other violence in the family, and there was less poverty. It might be that combined neglect and injury is particularly damaging to children's development, while injury alone has a better prognosis.

Age and sex

The ratio of male to female was 1.5:1 (Table 2.ii). NSPCC 1977–81 figures for all under-fives show a similar sex ratio and age-sex distribution. In the Glasgow series, however, the sex ratio was approximately equal.

Table 2.ii **Age and sex at registration**

Years	Male %	Female %	All %
Under one	27	33	30
one – two	44	41	42
three – five	29	26	28
N = 100%	101	69	170

Boys and girls were equally likely to be seriously injured. Under-ones were more likely to be uninjured – because some were placed on the register at birth after previous injury to siblings. One-to-two year olds were more likely to have other than 'slight' injuries – 60% had serious or moderate injuries compared to 32% of under-fives and 26% of three-to-fives. It has been suggested that this age might represent a period of particular stress in child rearing, when support from health services is less, playgroups are not available and children, still physically weak, are beginning to show more independence so that conflict with parents is more likely.

Perpetrators

The child's injury was inflicted by the female caregiver in 40% of cases; and by the male caregiver in 43%. Both male and female caregivers were believed to be involved (or it was unclear which of them was responsible) in another 11%. Outsiders were held responsible in 6%. These figures were similar to the NSPCC's for all its registers.

Father and mother figures acting separately were equally likely to inflict serious injury. When both parent figures, or outsiders, were involved, there was a significantly higher risk of more serious injury. Serious injury was most likely when the circumstances were obscure and responsibility denied.

Adults living with a child have most opportunity to inflict injury, so the perpetrator needs to be considered in relation to the nature of the household (Table 2.iii). In reconstituted families, a male parent figure was entirely or partly responsible for the injury in 50% of cases (37% in families where the two parents shared all the children).

A large amount of social data recorded and coded in 1981 still existed in NSPCC register forms at the time of the follow-up. Case conference minutes

Table 2.iii   **Household type and perpetrator of injury**

Perpetrator	Household				
	Lone %	Joint %	Reconstit %	Other %	All %
Female parent/ substitute	65	24	28	0	34
Male parent/ substitute	19	37	50	25	37
Both/either	5	10	11	25	10
Other	3	6	4	50	5
No injury	8	23	7	0	14
N = 100%	37	70	54	4	165

Data missing on 5 cases

and documents were nearly all still there. Four experienced social workers were employed and trained to abstract data from these documents onto a standard schedule. Data available on at least 85% of the sample were classified as follows:

1.   The abuse incident: whether the child was injured; the severity of injury; whether neglect was also mentioned; whether sex abuse was mentioned; who the perpetrator was; whether immediate protective action was taken; whether the case conference recommended care proceedings.

2.   The abused child: birthweight; birth problems; age when placed on register; occurrence of previous abuse; number of previous changes in household/address; previously in institution (including hospital) or foster home.

3.   The family and social background: whether the child was living with two birth parents; family dependent on welfare; number of poverty indicators recorded; domestic violence; abuse of siblings; criminal record of mother/father.

The next step was to test these possible predictors against the children's outcomes nine to ten years later. There were no very strong relationships between baseline variables and outcomes. Statistically significant associations were found between eight of the predictor variables and one or more outcome measures (table 2.v).

When physical neglect and inadequate parental care were mentioned in the 1981 records, the children nine to ten years later showed more behaviour problems at school, lower scores on the cognitive testing summary factor and had higher self-rated depression scores. Other research has found that early

Table 2.iv **Baseline characteristics of follow-up sample**

Abuse incident

% ever injured	88
% severe injury	13
% concurrent neglect	37
% concurrent sex abuse	3.5
% mother was perpetrator	33
% father was perpetrator	26
% cohab/step perpetrator	15
% perpetrator unclear	10
% immediate protective action	23
% care proceedings recommended	28

Abused child

% birthweight < 2000 gr.	8	
% birth problems/premature	37	
mean months at registration	23	
% abused once before	14	
% abused two + times before	11	
Mean previous household changes	2.4	(range 0–8)
% previous institution or foster care	19	

Family problems

% living with 2 birth parents	42	
% living with lone parent	20	
% reconstituted family	34	
% on welfare	67	
mean poverty indicators	1.9	(range 0–5)
% domestic violence	51	
% previous abuse of sibling	34	
Father criminal record for violence	25.5	
Father other criminal record	26	
Mother criminal record for violence	7	
Mother other criminal record	25	

neglect may have particularly damaging consequences for children's development (Egeland et al., 1983; Wodarski et al., 1990; Claussen & Crittenden, 1991).

Very few reports of sexual abuse were found in the 1981 records – reflecting the age of the children then as well the lower awareness of the problem. When sexual abuse was recorded as a possibility, the affected children nine to ten years later were showing more behaviour problems at home (not at school) and reported more problems in relationships with peers. They had lower scores on some cognitive tests.

Just as the spread of abuse may be important, so may its persistence. There was some evidence that children who had experienced persistent abuse by the time they were registered were showing reduced cognitive performance and had more problems with peers. However, there was no effect on the ratings of behaviour and altogether the relationship was a weak and inconsistent one.

Table 2.v **1981 predictors and outcomes**

Predictor	Parent behav. rating	Teacher behav. rating	Peer problems	Cognitive perf.	Child's depression score
Concurrent poss/def neglect		+ ⋆		+ ⋆	+ ⋆
Concurrent poss/def sex abuse	+ ⋆		+ ⋆	+ ⋆	
Child never injured					+ ⋆⋆
Father was perpetrator	− ⋆				
Child prev. inst/ foster care	+ ⋆				
Child prev. abused once				+ ⋆	
Child prev. abused twice or more			+ ⋆		
Concurrent domestic violence					+ ⋆
Sibs prev. abused					+ ⋆

One way analysis of variance
⋆ p < .05 + = positive association
⋆⋆ p < .01 − = negative association

Severity of injury had no association with outcomes but, against expectation, children who had never been injured but were registered because of fears for their safety had significantly raised depression scores.

Four children had serious injuries judged likely to have long-term effects on their brain or senses. Three of these were in special schools or had received statements of special educational needs by the time of follow-up, and the fourth showed effects in the form of very poor performance on the cognitive tests. Thus the very few children who received this type of serious injury did show specific effects on their cognitive development nine to ten years later.

When abuse took place in the context of other family violence – to siblings or spouses – children's depression scores nine to ten years later were significantly raised but there were no other effects.

Children who had been placed in institutions (including hospitals) or foster care before the index referral in 1981 were rated by parents as showing more behaviour problems at home. When the father was the perpetrator children had fewer behaviour problems at home. A possible explanation is that perpetrator-fathers were more likely to have left the household by the time of follow-up while perpetrator-mothers were more likely to be still living with their children and perhaps were intolerant of behaviour.

Low birthweight had no effect on the behavioural or cognitive outcomes but, not surprisingly, children who weighed less than 2,000 grammes at birth tended to be smaller and had significantly smaller head circumference measurements.

Multivariate analysis was undertaken to examine the effect of all the 1981 predictors upon the outcomes. Very little of the variance in any outcome measure was explained by the action of the 1981 predictors in combination.

It is unlikely, therefore, that the circumstances surrounding the abuse some ten years earlier and the family context then had a great deal of direct influence on the children's outcomes so long afterwards. There was certainly no evidence that injury in itself was important: in fact the children who had never been injured were more depressed and had no better outcomes in any respect. There was some evidence, though too much weight should not be put on it, that the combination of different kinds of abuse or of abuse and neglect had more serious longer-term consequences, and possibly so did persistent abuse. Thus, it could be cautiously stated that, if physical maltreatment is a one-off event, with no previous episodes involving the child or any siblings; if it is specific and there are no signs of associated physical neglect or suspected sexual abuse; if the family climate is not a generally violent one, then the prognosis for the child may be better. It could not be claimed that any of these factors, alone or in combination, have great predictive power in relation to individual children's development in the longer term.

Influence of circumstances at registration upon repetition of abuse

Even though the context of the original abuse had little or no predictive power in relation to longer-term outcomes, it might still be important in predicting repetition of harm. Repetition is discussed in more detail in the next chapter. Here we will only examine possible relationships between the baseline data items listed on page 29 and subsequent documented repetition.

Of the 144 children who were interviewed 26 (18%) suffered repeated injury that was documented in NSPCC, health or social services records. More of the children who were not interviewed (31%) suffered repeated injury, giving a total re-injury rate of 20%. This is on the low side when compared with other results (Gibbons et al., 1994; Farmer & Owen, 1993). It is a minimum estimate since only incidents clearly identified as abusive in records were counted. Eight children (out of the total sample of 170) were sexually abused during the follow-up, two of whom were also re-injured.

We compared the re-abused children with those who had not been re-abused on each of the baseline data items. A weak relationship was found with only one item – the original perpetrator's being the mother (p > .05). The circumstances in which abuse occurred, therefore, did not seem useful predictors of the child's subsequent safety. This is probably because registration, and still more any signs of repetition, leads to many changes in the child's environment – such as removal from home, break-up of the original family, move to a new area and so on. The circumstances that existed at the time of the abuse are not stable and probably exercise little continuing influence.

Chapter 3

Events in the lives of abused children: effects on outcome

Influences of the past

Life events are defined as any event or change in an individual's life which could be thought to have a significant effect upon that individual's psychosocial adjustment. Events like hospitalisation, the birth or death of family members and home moves, often represent periods of dramatic and stressful change in a person's life. The review of the literature (Part 3) showed that there may be many factors involved in explaining the impact of life events upon individual adjustment, and that their impact may be short or long term.

One of the areas to have received least attention in terms of research is the role of events and changes in the lives of abused children and their families. Many surveys, eg Creighton and Noyes (1989), have recorded the chaotic level of change and numerous stressful incidents experienced within abusing families but the impact of this lifestyle, upon both children and parents, is more assumed than proven. This is an important omission in several respects: firstly, life events include incidents of abuse to a child. The current study set out to examine the effect of both abuse and subsequent professional intervention upon children's developmental competencies. Unfortunately, the registration of the children in 1981 did not preclude further incidents of abuse. Subsequent incidents of abuse are of importance both for their effect upon children's outcome and also as a measure of the effectiveness of the interventions received by registered children. Secondly, life events include a number of other adversities and changes which could be thought to have an effect upon children's developmental competencies. Children who change schools frequently may suffer in terms of their educational attainment; numerous changes of address may make it far more difficult for a child to make friends and leave them isolated both in their neighbourhood and at school.

Methodology

Data on life events were obtained through searches of social work, community health and hospital records. The main function of these records was to log professional interventions and to chart the development of a child, and his or her family, in terms of professional concerns, be they social or medical. However, these records also contained a considerable amount of information on life events. The complete list of life events for which this study attempted to gather information on is given in Table 3.i.

There were two other sources of life events data. The first of these was a questionnaire to teachers, which asked for details of the child's schooling history eg number of schools previously attended and special educational needs. A second, albeit somewhat limited, source of life events data was provided through the tracing process. This source was particularly valuable in helping to calculate the number of addresses and moves which a family had had. Through tracing it was also possible to obtain some very basic information on the families who refused to participate in the research eg type of accommodation and caregiving situation.

Table 3.i **Complete list of life events**

On the index child:	subsequent incident of physical abuse
	subsequent incidents of sexual abuse
	attendance at nursery school
	attendance at primary school
	attendance at secondary school
	attendance at special school
	other special educational provision
	suspensions or expulsions from school
	separations from caregivers
	separations from siblings
	other injuries to child
	neurological damage
	hospitalisation
	serious illness
	changes of address
On the index child's siblings:	subsequent incidents of physical abuse
	subsequent incidents of sexual abuse
	births
	deaths
	other injuries
	serious illness
	hospitalisation
On the index child's caregivers:	serious illness
	general hospitalisation
	psychiatric hospitalisation
	self-harm
	death

The choice of which life events to collect data on was based upon two main criteria. Firstly, the event was identified by the literature as being of potential importance in terms of children's developmental competencies. Secondly, there had to be a good chance that the event would have been systematically entered into the records held by professional workers. This meant that some events, such as unemployment of caregivers, had to be left out, as it was felt that professionals might not regularly record such events.

The vast majority of life events data came from records. This means that the data are susceptible to all the vagaries of the recording process; an event may not be known to the person completing the record, and the professional concerned may decide not to record the event or may record the event in a biased or inaccurate manner. Records also go missing and this can have a major bearing upon the overall quality of the data which are available for analysis.

Given the inevitable question mark over the reliability of record data, it needs to be remembered throughout the following discussion that the figures presented are minimum counts: it is possible that the actual incidence and prevalence for given life events were higher than is indicated by these figures. However, we can be more-or-less certain that the actual rates were no lower than these figures indicate. Similarly a guarantee can be given that a specific event did occur – if it is in the record – but we cannot be so sure that an event did not occur, simply because it was not found in the record.

By looking at the relationship between the frequency of events and the existence of particular records, or the degree of contact contained in the record, it is possible to shed some light on the degree to which records are influencing the quantity of the life events data. It is reasonable to expect that as the number of family-professional contacts increased, so would the recording of the number of life events. Conversely, it is reasonable to expect that as the frequency of life events increased so would the number of family-professional contacts. The relationship between record availability and the frequency of life events is examined later in this chapter.

Subsequent incidents of physical abuse of the Index Children

The literature suggests that between one-quarter and one-third of children are re-abused after they come to the attention of child protection agencies. In the review of the literature in Part 3 it is argued that there are a number of methodological problems with much of the existing work on this topic, which cast doubt on the reliability of these findings. The importance of reliable information on the number and types of children, who are most at risk of subsequent abuse, cannot be overstated. These data are relevant in terms of children's safety and the general effectiveness of the child protection service. Subsequent incidents of abuse are also important in terms of the relationship they may have with children's developmental outcomes.

Two points need to be borne in mind when considering the figures which follow. Firstly, the reports of subsequent incidents of abuse were taken directly from the records. The persons responsible for searching records did not attempt to interpret any events described in the record. Only incidents which were clearly described as abuse, by the professional who completed the record, were included in this analysis. Incidents where there was an indeterminate diagnosis, or no diagnosis at all, were excluded from the category 'subsequent abuse'.

The second point is that the incidents described here are correctly referred to as subsequent ones ie subsequent to the registration of the index child. The figures represented here do not refer to a 're-abuse' rate as this implies that all the children concerned were abused at the baseline point and, as we have seen in chapter 2, a small proportion was not injured in 1981.

By the end of the follow-up period, which was a maximum of 10 years for any child in the study, 20% of the sample were known to have been physically abused after having been registered in 1981 (N = 34). One of these children was known to have been abused on two separate occasions. Only three of the incidents were serious, using NSPCC criteria.

Table 3.ii gives a breakdown of the time between registration and subsequent injury for these 34 children. All the life events data were originally coded according to the age of the child in completed years. This explains why there is an apparent increase in the incidence between the first and second birthdays after registration. Whereas all the periods after the first subsequent birthday cover 12 months, the period between registration and the first subsequent birthday is anything between 1 and 364 days. If registration occurs randomly in terms of the number of months elapsed since a child's previous birthday then this first period probably covers the equivalent of only

Table 3.ii   **Time lapse between registration and subsequent injury**

	Subsequent physical abuse incidents	
Completed age year	**N**	**%**
Same age year as at registration	10	29
1 age year after registration	16	46
2 age year after registration	5	14
3 age year after registration	2	6
4 age year after registration	1	3
5 age year after registration	1	3
6 age year after registration	0	0
7 age year after registration	0	0
	35	101

*Does not equal 100 because of rounding

6 months. So the actual incidence in the first period may be twice that which is shown in Table 3.ii.

Table 3.ii shows that subsequent incidents of physical abuse are far more likely to occur within a relatively short time of registration. Over three-quarters of all incidents took place before the children's second consecutive birthday since registration, which is equivalent to a maximum period of two years.

The dramatic decrease in the incidence of subsequent abuse is probably due to a number of factors. Over time an increasing proportion of the families ceased to have social work involvement. As the children got older contact with other agencies, particularly health visitors, also diminished. With less professional contact there would have been less opportunity for injuries to be detected. With increasing age the children would also have been at less risk of being physically abused (Creighton and Noyes, 1989). The number of children permanently removed from home, whether through adoption, fostering or being placed in residential care, also increased over time. As these children were being removed from a high risk environment, again this should have led to a decrease in the number of subsequent incidents of physical abuse.

Data presented later in this chapter suggests that over time many of the families were becoming far more stable. This is noticeable in terms of the number of home moves, changes of school and a number of other factors which are discussed below. Therefore, one of the reasons for the fall off in the rate of subsequent physical abuse may be the increasing stability of families over time. The increase in the stability of families may have been due to factors within the family itself, eg parents becoming older and more mature, and also to the time which it took for intervention to have an effect. Therefore, it may be unrealistic to expect abusing parents to change their behaviour within a few months. Corby (1987), found that there was an optimum treatment time of between 7 and 18 months, so it may be that intervention had to extend over many months, if not a few years, before it began to alter family dynamics.

The figures presented here concur with those of the NSPCC, which show an equally dramatic decline over time in the incidence of subsequent physical abuse (Creighton and Noyes, 1989).

If the subsequent incidents are analysed by the children's status at registration ie abused versus cases of grave concern, then there is little difference between the groups in terms of the risk of subsequent incidents. 20% of those who were registered for physical abuse were subsequently harmed compared to 21% of those originally registered for 'grave concern'.

The sample consisted of a higher proportion of boys than girls, 56% and 44% respectively, which is normal amongst registered children of this age ie under 5 years at the time of registration (Creighton and Noyes, 1989). 22% of the girls, and 19% of the boys were known to have experienced a further incident of physical abuse. The findings suggest that the factors which explain the differential risk level for boys and girls in the general population may have been less significant in terms of subsequently abused children. It may be that these latter children come from particularly deviant families where boys and girls are equally at risk.

Subsequent incidents of sexual abuse

The children in the current study were registered in 1981, at a time when sexual abuse was not a criterion for registration. By the mid-1980s there was much greater professional awareness of this form of abuse. The number of known cases rose dramatically and sexual abuse became a criterion for registration. At the end of the follow-up, eight of the 169 living children were known to have been sexually abused, which is a prevalence of 4.7%.

It might be argued that the prevalence found in this study is not unexpectedly high, given the figures obtained in major prevalence surveys. However, it is important to point out that these figures were not based upon a self-report survey but are derived from officially identified cases. If the current sample had been asked directly about whether they had been sexually abused, it is possible that a much higher rate would have been obtained. It is also worth pointing out that the eight cases of sexual abuse tended to involve more serious types of sexual abuse.

Table 3.iii shows that, in keeping with other surveys, girls are highly over-represented amongst the children who were sexually abused. Detailed and reliable information regarding other aspects of this form of subsequent abuse were not readily available. This was due to a number of reasons. Firstly, some of the children were relatively young when the abuse occurred, and the records showed that they found it difficult to provide precise information concerning when the abuse began and how frequently it occurred. The records themselves tended to concentrate upon the first incident to be officially detected. The impression which emerges from the records is that the children were abused across quite a wide range of ages and that there was no particular pattern in terms of time since registration. However, as the numbers are so small it is not possible to make very reliable statements as to trends in the data.

Possibly the most reliable data concerning this form of subsquent abuse relates to the perpetrators. Table 3.iii gives the relationship between the child and the perpetrator.

In only one of these eight cases was there any overlap between the perpetrators of the physical abuse, in 1981, and the perpetrators of the subsequent sexual abuse. Even in this single case, it was not certain as to whether the physical abuse was carried out by the birth father (who was known to have carried out the sexual abuse) or by the child's birth mother.

Table 3.iii **Perpetrators of subsequent incidents of sexual abuse**

Child	Perpetrator
boy	natural father
boy	natural father
girl	older brother
girl	male babysitter
girl	grandfather and his friend
girl	social worker and three family acquaintances
girl	unknown
girl	unknown

These figures suggest that some abused children live in environments which are characterised not by a single deviant individual ie caregiver, nor by a deviant caregiver–child relationship, but more by a culture of deviancy. In such situations the child may be exposed to several different forms of abuse, instigated by more than one abuser.

Two of the eight children who were known to have been subsequently sexually abused, were also physically abused after registration. Therefore the total number of all children who experienced physical, sexual or both of these forms of abuse after registration was 40, or 24% of the sample.

Subsequent abuse of siblings

During the course of compiling the life events data, information was also collected on the subsequent abuse of siblings. In order to ensure that the collection of this information was more systematic and reliable, only full and half-siblings who were resident with the index child at the time of the subsequent abuse have been included in this analysis.

Information relating to siblings was obtained through the search of records during the main course of the study. There was no separate search of specific sibling records.

For social work records this was not so important as often there was a single file for the whole family. Where individuals in the same family did have their own file then information was usually duplicated within all the files. By contrast, community health and hospital records referred only to the individual child. By searching only the records of the index child there is bound to be a loss of data concerning siblings. However, all the life events relating to siblings and parents are of such significance that there is a good chance that they would be recorded in the files of all family members. Furthermore, as the information in this analysis was derived from a number of separate sources, there was less likelihood of information being lost. Having said this, it is important to reiterate an earlier point; namely, that the figures presented here are minimum counts. We cannot be certain whether the true incidence and prevalence of the life events covered in this discussion are higher than we have found but we do know that they cannot be any lower.

Sibling life events were only included if they occurred when the index child and the sibling were living with one another. There were two reasons for this policy: firstly if we had included events which occurred when the children were living apart from one another this would have made data collection very unsystematic, as the chances of actually obtaining such information would vary enormously from one case to another. As already stated, there is a degree of unreliability in the data but to have included life events on non-resident siblings would have involved an unacceptable level of unreliability. Secondly, one of the main purposes for studying life events was for their effect on the outcome, particularly in terms of developmental competencies, of the index children. If a sibling experienced a particular life event while living in a different household from the index child, it is difficult to argue that the event had an impact upon the index child.

24% of the index children (N = 41) had not lived with a full or half-sibling during the course of the follow-up. The remaining 129 index children had a total of 253 siblings living with them between registration and the outcome stage of the project. Of these 253 siblings only 14 were known to have been physically abused after the registration of the index child. This is a prevalence of 6%, compared to a prevalence for subsequent physical abuse to the index children of 20%. Even allowing for a loss of data on the siblings and the exclusion of non-resident siblings the size of the difference between the two groups of children is striking. This finding adds weight to the 'special victim' model of child abuse (Gil, 1970) which holds that characteristics of particular children in a sibship render them more likely to be abused. In terms of treatment, especially that aimed at preventing further abuse, it would seem that efforts may need to be directed at the relationship between the caregivers and particular children in the family. At the same time it must be remembered that almost one-quarter of the sample did not have any siblings and that in some families the index child was not alone in being abused. Therefore the explanation of abuse may vary between families, which again emphasises the importance of distinguishing between different groups of abusing families.

Only two of the 253 siblings were known to have been sexually abused after the registration of the index child. This is a prevalence of 1%, as against 5% for the index children. This reinforces the idea that in some families particular children within a sibship may be singled out for abuse. Again there may have been bias in the data in that, for example, once a child was registered s/he received greater professional attention, whereby subsequent incidents were more likely to have been detected. Siblings who were not on the register may have experienced the same rate of subsequent abuse, but less may have been detected because they were under less scrutiny. However, given that the incidents of sexual abuse tended to be towards the more serious end of the spectrum, there was less likelihood that detection bias would have had much of a role. Similarly, given the seriousness with which sexual abuse is handled by child protection agencies and the fact that the incidents described here were generally more serious forms of sexual abuse, the limited access to sibling files was probably not a significant factor in terms of the difference in prevalence between the two groups of children. The event was likely to be recorded in all the families' files, particularly in the case of social work files. It appears then that registered children are more likely to be sexually abused than their siblings.

There were a total of 16 incidents of subsequent physical or sexual abuse to siblings after the registration of the index child. One sibling was both physically and sexually abused, so the total number of abused siblings was 15. In four of these cases the corresponding index child was also the victim of a subsequent abuse incident. This means that subsequent abuse occurred in the families of a further 11 index children. Therefore, subsequent incidents of abuse occurred in 30% (N = 51) of the index children's families.

It has been noted that no subsequent incident of physical abuse was recorded for any index children beyond the 6th consecutive birthday since registration. (It was difficult to obtain reliable data for the onset and cessation times of the sexual abuse incidents but they appeared to be distributed fairly randomly.) The absence of physical abuse incidents in the second half of the period covered by the follow-up is obviously to be welcomed. However, that physical injuries, though rarely serious, occurred in almost one-third of the families after placement of a child on the register is worrying. It may be that abusive behaviour is so entrenched that it takes a considerable amount of intervention in order to curtail it.

Finally it should be remembered that some children have, in principle at least, not been exposed to the risk of subsequent abuse for part, if not all, of the follow-up period because they have been placed in substitute care. Obviously children in residential care or foster care, or in adoptive homes, can be abused. However, one would hope that the risk is much lower than that in the homes from which the children came. This raised two important points: firstly, that the prevalence was based on a risk period which was less than 10 years for each child. Secondly, not all of the 162 families could have contributed to these figures, as some children were permanently removed at the time of the registration or shortly after. So if, for example, children who were placed in care at the time of registration were excluded, the prevalence would be even higher. The safety of children in new families is further examined in chapter 6.

These figures for subsequent abuse of index children and siblings may call into question the effectiveness of intervention strategies, particularly in terms of preventing further abuse. Alternatively it could be said that the figures reflect how resistant to change is this form of behaviour.

Relationship between life events and outcome

We examined the relationship between children's scores on the measures of developmental competencies and the life events they had experienced. Our expectation was that the more turbulence, changes and separations a child had experienced, the poorer the child's performance was likely to be.

Subsequent incidents of physical abuse were recorded to one-fifth of the sample. It could be hypothesised that if physical abuse did have a direct effect upon outcome, then it would have been more evident in these children. Similarly, a subsequent incident of physical abuse could be taken as symptomatic of more severe problems in either the caregiver, or in the caregiver-child relationship, both of which could lead to poorer outcome. Therefore, plausible arguments can be made for a relationship between subsequent physical abuse and poorer outcome.

In fact, no relationships were found between subsequent abuse and scores on the four separate outcome factors – behaviour at home and school, cognitive test performance and depression – nor problems with peers. Table 3.iv divides up all the children whom it had been possible to assign to one of the three summary outcome clusters into those who experienced a subsequent incident of physical abuse and those who did not.

Table 3.iv **Relationship between subsequent physical abuse and outcome cluster**

	Outcome cluster					
	Poor		Good		Low performance	
Subsequent physical abuse	N	%	N	%	N	%
No	45	43	24	23	36	34
Yes	9	37	4	17	11	46
All	54	42	28	22	47	36

Chi square 1.1 df2 sig .55

Children who experienced subsequent abuse were slightly, but not significantly less likely to have a good overall outcome. As the findings stand, it appears that subsequent physical abuse only marginally increases the risk of a poorer outcome. In some ways this could have been anticipated from the distribution of the sample described in Chapter 1. When compared to the Comparison group it was clear that the Index group had worse outcomes but the differences were not as great as might have been expected, and a majority of the index group were in the intermediate or good outcome group. Therefore neither abuse nor subsequent abuse, taken on their own may be very predictive in terms of outcome.

Child sexual abuse is widely believed to predict particularly adverse outcomes across a variety of developmental competencies. Although the number of children who suffered sexual abuse in the current sample was very small (N = 8), the potential consequences of this form of abuse are so great that it is important to determine whether it had any effect on outcome.

Four children (half those sexually abused) were in the good outcome cluster – a higher proportion than in the sample as a whole. It has to be acknowledged straight away that this analysis is based upon very small numbers, and not too much can be inferred from it. All that can be said is that in this study there were no evidence that sexual abuse necessarily led to poor outcome for children in the longer term.

Outcome profiles were based upon a number of quite different developmental competencies such as behaviour, cognitive ability and depression. However, a fixed number of measures was used so it is possible that the sexually abused children were experiencing negative sequelae which were simply not covered. In looking at the relationship between abuse and outcome, no allowance has been made for mediating factors such as victim-perpetrator age difference, or victim-perpetrator relationship. Therefore this finding needs to be treated with caution. What may have been happening in some of the cases of sexual abuse is that the child may have, in effect, 'localised' the damage caused by the abuse, such that one area of their development was impaired but the remainder was left intact.

All injuries which had not clearly been caused by abuse were put together in a general category of 'other injuries'. There is a good chance that some of these injuries had, in fact, been the result of abuse. Some of the injuries were attributable to parental neglect of young children, whereas some older children were putting themselves in dangerous situations. Other injuries were straightforward accidents eg children tripping over at school. Children who had no subsequent other injury over the follow-up period were compared to those children who had one or more of these injuries. Consistent with the findings for subsequent physical injury and sexual abuse, there were no significant differences in the outcomes of those who experienced other injuries and those who did not.

Hospital Admission

The registered children were, almost by definition, very likely to be admitted to hospital. However, injuries were not the only reason for admittance to hospital. Some children, particularly the very young ones were, on occasions, admitted because of their parents' inability or unwillingness to care for them. Other children were admitted because of long-term illness. The children who suffered neurological damage were also admitted to hospital more frequently. As with 'other injuries', hospital admission had diverse origins. A breakdown of hospital admittance by outcome group is given in Table 3.v.

Table 3.v   **The effects of hospital admission upon outcome**

	Separate hospital admissions									
	0		**1**		**2**		**3**		**4**	
Outcome group	**N**	**%**	**N**	**%**	**N**	**%**	**N**	**%**	**N**	**%**
Good	6	16	7	15	5	33	5	33	6	50
Low	14	37	14	30	7	47	5	33	2	17
Poor	18	47	26	55	3	20	5	33	4	33

Children who had not been admitted to hospital during the follow-up period had a distribution of outcomes which were quite similar to that of the children who had been admitted only once. The most striking feature of these figures is that children who had been 2, 3 or 4 or more times had better outcomes. This finding holds if the groups are collapsed eg 15% of children who were admitted to hospital never or only once were in the good outcome group, compared to 38% of the children who had been admitted on two or more occasions. It is difficult to explain this finding. Hospital admission is probably related to a whole host of other factors such as general health status and home conditions. It could be that admittance to hospital was a product, in part, of a better level of care at home which included attention to children's health needs. There was anecdotal evidence to suggest that some children welcomed admission to hospital. Consequently it is difficult to suggest reasons for this finding, but what does seem reasonably clear is that admission to hospital, which was probably more common for this group than the norm, made little contribution to negative outcome.

No new incidents of neurological damage were noted after registration. Only 12 episodes of serious illness (defined as requiring the child to be in bed) were recorded throughout the follow-up period. Identifying such episodes was difficult and the small number of incidents made analysis, in terms of effect upon outcome, unreliable. It is interesting though that the children did not appear to be particularly badly afflicted by serious illness. Having said this, the records did give the impression that less severe ailments such as hearing and visual impairments, heart murmurs, and epilepsy, were quite common. One wonders whether some of these eg hearing and visual impairments were related to previous physical abuse.

Changes in caregiver

The number of separate caregiver episodes each child had during each age year after registration was coded. Each episode had to have a minimum duration of one month before it was included in the analysis. This led, inevitably, to a loss of some caregiving episodes but some cut-off had to be used in order to exclude episodes which were not really part of a caregiving relationship eg a two week holiday with grandparents. It was also felt that for the caregiving episode to have any impact upon the child, it would have to be of sufficient duration – judged in this case, albeit arbitrarily, to be one month or more.

Excluded from this analysis are those caregiving episodes which were part of being 'in care' ie residential and foster care, and adoption. The complete list of caregiving episodes to be included in this analysis are as follows:

Both birth parents
Birth mother alone
Birth father alone
Birth mother plus father substitute
Birth father plus mother substitute
Grandparent(s) alone (not fostering)
Other relatives alone (not fostering)
Friends alone
Other eg spending parts of the week with different parents

Each time a child spent one month or more in any of these caregiving arrangements it was coded as one episode.

The results showed no clear relationship between the number of caregiver episodes and the child's outcome in the longer term. There are several reasons for believing that the number of caregiving episodes should relate to outcome, such as the problems associated with separation and with forming relationships with new caregivers. From the figures it appears that a straight-forward relationship between the number of episodes and outcomes should not be assumed. It may be that the type and quality of the caregiving relationship were more important than the number of changes. It should also be pointed out that many of the changes in caregiving arrangements took place between a restricted number of caregivers, for example, a child who

Table 3.vi **Relationship between the number of separate caregiver episodes and outcome**

Outcome group	Separate number of caregiver episodes					
	< 11		11–12		> 12	
	N	%	N	%	N	%
Good	14	25	7	20	8	20
Low	15	27	12	35	16	40
Poor	27	48	15	44	16	40

(*Does not equal 100 because of rounding)

spent a few months with grandparents and then the same length of time with a single parent, with this pattern being regularly repeated over a number of years, such that the number of episodes is high but the change in type of caregiving arrangement is low. Therefore the number of episodes on their own do exaggerate the amount of change experienced.

Number of different male and female caregivers

A child who moves from household to household, as some in the sample did, experiences repeated changes of caregiver. Since separations and changes in early childhood are believed to have a profound effect upon child development we expected that the more male and female caregivers a child had, the poorer would be the outcome. However, as with the number of caregiving episodes, no significant associations could be found with any of the individual outcomes measures nor with the summary outcome factors and clusters.

The children varied widely in how much instability and change they experienced. The mean number of female caregivers was 2.1 (range 1–8); and the mean number of male caregivers was 2.3 (range 0–7). Thus some children had as many as seven or eight changes during the follow up. The differences may be illustrated by examples.

Case 39 was placed on the register when he was nearly two. He had been removed to a foster home under a Place of Safety Order and remained there for some weeks before returning to mother and stepfather. Soon afterwards mother took him to a refuge to escape her partner's violence. He then stayed with his aunt before returning again to the family home. A new baby was born the next year (he was by now three) and he was moved again to another foster home to relieve stress on mother. After he was returned home mother again left with the children for the refuge. She returned home and the partner briefly left. There were several other moves between refuge, home and relatives over the next year, at the end of which the whole family moved to a new house. Child 39 was taken into care briefly and went to a children's home when another baby was born. He then spent further time with his aunt before being sent to a foster home. By the time he was five he had experienced 5 changes of female caregiver and 17 changes of residence. Yet at the time of follow-up, when he was 11, he was living with mother and the other children and his performance on the measures of developmental competence placed him in our good outcome cluster.

Case 2, *by contrast, who was placed on the register before the age of one year, remained with his parents for the whole period and only had four changes of residence. His scores on the outcome measures at follow-up placed him in the low performance cluster.*

These examples chosen at random merely illustrate the point that there was no simple association between early disruptive experiences and children's behaviour, peer relationships and educational attainment some years later. Some children appeared incredibly resilient and were apparently able to develop fairly normally despite very difficult early years.

Separation from siblings

The next life event-outcome relationship to be investigated was that of separation between the index child and his/her siblings. The distribution of outcomes is analysed separately for temporary separation (minimum one month) and permanent separations. The results are given in Table 3.vii.

Table 3.vii **The relationship between Index-sibling separations and outcome**

Outcome group	No temporary separation		One or more temporary separation		No permanent separation		One or more permanent separation	
	N	%	N	%	N	%	N	%
Good	19	20	9	30	21	20	7	35
Low	28	29	14	47	35	33	7	35
Poor	49	51	7	23	50	47	6	30
All	96	100	30	100	106	100	20	100

Again there were no significant relationships, but there was a tendency for Index children who experienced temporary separations from their siblings, and those who experienced permanent separations, to have better outcomes. It seems unlikely that there was a directly benefical effect in separating siblings – at least in terms of the index child's outcome, but there was no evidence (on our measures) of damaging effects in the longer term. Again the relationship between life events and outcome has been shown to be far more complicated, with no straightforward relationship between these two variables.

Health of caregivers

The number of caregivers who experienced serious ill-health or who were admitted to general hospital was very small. The outcomes for children whose parents had been ill or in hospital was found to be very similar to the remaining children in the sample, but being based on very small numbers, the findings were not very reliable. Similarly the number of children who had a caregiver admitted to psychiatric hospital was very small. However, it is perhaps worth noting that none of the children in the good outcome group had a caregiver admitted to psychiatric hospital, compared to a prevalence of 2% (N = 1) in the intermediate group and 7% (N = 4) in the poor outcome group.

Moves between places of residence

The final variable to be analysed in this group of 'domestic life' events was that of home moves. Any period of one week or more in duration, at one address, was counted as a period of residence. The total number of moves between such places of residence in each age year was coded for every child.

Contrary to expectation, there were no statistically significant relationships between the number of moves experienced by a child and his or her outcome on any of the measures.

Number of school changes

Similarly, no clear relationships were found between number of changes in primary school and outcomes.

Table 3.viii gives the distribution of outcome groups for children broken down by the total number of separate primary school episodes over the follow-up period.

Children with less than seven changes did better, but if the primary school frequency groups are collapsed into 1–7 episodes and 8+ episodes, then the differences between the two groups are very slight. Changes of primary school may not have been very detrimental to developmental competencies. It may be that it is the context of change which is important rather than the number of changes.

Too few children attended special schools or received special tuition or were excluded from school, for any reliable within-group comparisons. Just under one-third of the sample (N = 52) were attending mainstream secondary schools. Children in the good outcome cluster had experienced

Table 3.viii **The relationship between primary school episodes and outcome**

Outcome group	1–6		7		8		9+	
	N	%	N	%	N	%	N	%
Good	6	40	4	11	9	23	8	24
Low	5	33	13	37	9	23	14	41
Poor	4	27	18	51	21	54	12	35
All	15	100	35	99	39	100	34	100

somewhat fewer changes of secondary school (a mean of 2.3) than had children in the low performance group (2.8) or those with a poor overall outcome (2.9). So it may be that school changes have more effect at a later stage of children's lives.

The incidence of life events over time

In the earlier analysis of subsequent incidents of physical abuse it was found that there was a dramatic decline in the incidence for this particular life event.

Approximately three-quarters of all the incidents occurred within two years of registration and none were recorded more than six years after registration.

The decline in the incidence may have been due, in part, to the fact that over time an increasing number of children were de-registered, ceased to have social work intervention and no longer had contact with health visitors. Similarly, over time an increasing proportion of children had been removed from their original home and placed in substitute care. Therefore, the fall-off may have been due to decreased detection or the removal of the children from the high-risk environment. However, given that the large majority of children actually remained at home and that some subsequent incidents of sexual abuse came to professional attention in the latter half of the follow-up period, these factors may have had a limited role. A more significant factor may have been an increasing stabilisation of families over time. There are several reasons for believing that the reduction in the incidence of subsequent physical abuse over time was due to factors within the family. As parents aged and matured they may have been better able to handle the stresses of life in general, and child care in particular, without resorting to excessive corporal punishment. Research has shown that older children – who presumably have older parents – are at a lower risk of physical abuse (Creighton and Noyes, 1989).

Further evidence for the stabilisation of families over time comes from an analysis of other life events. The life events chosen for this particular analysis were those for which there was the most reliable date. As caregiver arrange-ments (excluding substitute care), home moves and school attendance constituted basic information for service providers, it was felt that these would have been recorded very accurately in the files, enhanced through the tracing process also through the teacher questionnaire (which noted recent address and numbers of schools attended).

All these life events showed a constant decline over time. The figures for primary school episodes appeared to go against this trend, but this was only because the sample was aged under 5 at the time of registration. As they aged they entered primary school thereby inflating these figures. By year 6, when the entire sample was of primary school age, the figures peak and then begin to decline, down to year 10 when children started entering secondary school.

In terms of subsequent physical abuse and home caregiving episodes (having allowed for age) it is clear that the registered children experienced greater stability with time. It may have been that intervention took many years to have an effect or that it was not until the parents were much older that they could offer their children greater stability.

Reliability of data

The vast majority of the life events data was obtained from the searches of social work, community health and hospital records. As the records were compiled for the purposes of on-going practice, with no reference to research considerations, there was a question mark over the reliability of the data. As there were different numbers and types of records available for each child, this concern was even greater. This is the reason for emphasising that while the true incidence and prevalence of life events may have been higher than those found in this study, they were almost certainly no lower.

The greatest amount of professional contact the families had was with social work agencies. In many cases this consisted of quite regular contact over several years. Community health records usually detailed numerous family-professional contacts, but far fewer than the social work records. By comparison with social work and community health records, hospital records contained very few descriptions of family-professional contacts. It was assumed, therefore, that the frequency of life events provided by each record would be greatest for social work files and lowest for hospital notes, with community health records occupying an intermediate position in this order. Similarly it was assumed that as the number of different records available for each child increased, so would the number of life events.

If record availability had an effect upon the frequency of life events, it would be most noticeable in terms of the social work (S/S) and community health (C/H) records, as these contained far more information than the hospital records. Table 3.ix divides the sample into four groups, according to

Table 3.ix **The relationship between record availability and the prevalence of subsequent physical abuse and 'other injuries'**

| | Subsequently | | | | |
| | All | Physically abused | | 'Other' injured | |
Record category	N	N	%	N	%
Both S/W and C/H record	107	24	22	69	64
Only S/W record	47	13	28	25	53
Only C/H record	7	1	14	5	71
Neither S/W or C/H record	11	0	0	6	55

record availability. The frequency of a number of different life events was examined to see whether the records had an effect. An attempt was made to use a number of quite different life events and also life events which occurred quite frequently, as it was felt that this would be a more comprehensive test as to whether record availability had an effect.

The group for whom it had been possible to search only the social work record had, contrary to expectations, the highest prevalence for subsequent abuse (28%). The absence of a community health record was often tied to the fact that a child had left the study area, to be followed by his/her record. The earlier a child left the study area the more likely was his/her record to be passed onto the new health district. Therefore, children with only a social work record may be over-represented by the more mobile families. The greater 'instability' of these families may have been linked to a higher risk of subsequent physical abuse to the index child. Whatever the reason for the difference in prevalence between these two groups it is clear that greater availability of records does not necessarily equate with more life events.

The above finding is reversed for the prevalence of 'other' subsequent injuries. Whereas almost two thirds of children with both social work and community health records were noted to have had at least one such subsequent injury, the rate for the group with only social work records was just over 50%. The figures for subsequent physical abuse suggested that individual cases may exert a greater effect upon prevalence than record availability. The figures for subsequent other injuries suggests that the effect of record availability may vary with different life events. Subsequent physical abuse was probably recorded more reliably across all records because of its implications. Accidental injuries, by contrast, may have come to the attention of a health visitor or school doctor, and have been recorded in community health records but their occurrence may not have been passed onto key social workers.

It was difficult to detect any definite trends amongst children for whom there was only the community health record or neither of the two records covered in this analysis. There was a suggestion that the absence of these records leads to an underestimation of the prevalence of subsequent physical abuse. No such incidents were recorded amongst the 11 children where neither the social work nor the community health record had been found. Conversely, both of these latter groups had high prevalence for other injuries. (The data on other injuries to the group with neither social work nor community health records, were obtained from hospital records). The numbers of children and life events in these two record categories were too small to be very reliable, but the figures may be taken as further, albeit tentative, evidence that there was not a simple relationship between the amount of record data and the number of life events.

The relationship between record availability and life events was also looked at in terms of the mean number of episodes at primary school, the number of caregiver episodes and the mean number of home moves experienced by the four record groups over the follow-up period.

The figures in Table 3.x suggest that the children and families for whom only the social work record was searched may have been more deviant than the sample overall. Table 3.ix showed that they were more likely to be subsequently abused than children in any other group. The figures in Table 3.x indicate that these children changed school and home address more frequently than those children for whom both records were available. However, of these two groups the 'both records' category had the greater number of changes in caregiving situation (excluding substitute care placements). There is evidence in the figures for a reduction in the frequency of life events, as the number and quality of records searched decline: the group with only community health records had only 5.6 primary school episodes and 4.0 home moves over the follow-up period. In terms of the mean number of caregiving episodes, the picture is reversed, with this group having a mean

Table 3.x **The relationship between record availability and life events frequency**

Record category		Mean number of episodes		
	N	Primary school	Caregiver	Home moves
Both S/W and C/H record	107	7.4	10.7	5.0
Only S/W record	47	7.6	8.6	8.6
Only C/H record	7	5.6	11.0	4.0
Neither S/W or C/H record	11	7.9	12.4	1.0

number of 11.0 such episodes over the follow-up period, while the equivalent figure for the 'no records' group was 12.4.

In conclusion it can be said that some life events may increase as the number of records available for searching increases. However, the record category in which a child is located may have masked differences between cases. Perhaps the best example of this was seen in the cases of children for whom only the community health record or no record had been found. Despite the limited amount of information on these children, the frequency of some life events was quite high. It may have been that records were more difficult to find for the more deviant families. When a record was found for such a family it often revealed a high level of change, eg primary school episodes and caregiver episodes. Social work records appeared to be the greatest source of life events data but there is no simple and clear-cut relationship between record availability and the number of life events.

Conclusion

In summary, no clearcut relationships were found between the children's performance on measures of developmental competencies at follow-up and the number of life events of various sorts that were noted in health, social services and educational records. Specifically, the occurrence of subsequent physical or sexual abuse or of 'accidental' injuries had no significant association with the child's outcome. Nor did the number of separate caregiving episodes, nor the number of different female or male carers nor the number of moves of residence. These results were so contrary to expectation that a possible explanation must be the unreliability of the agency records. When this explanation was tested it did not seem to be sufficient, but a question mark must remain over the negative findings.

Information about the context in which the events occurred, and the meaning of them to the child and adults involved, was lacking due to the retrospective nature of the study. It may be that these qualitative aspects are far more important than the absolute number of events or the type of event. However, just as we found in the previous chapter that the severity of the original injury (apart from the few extreme cases), or even whether the child had been injured at all, had little bearing upon outcome, so we have found in this chapter that repetition of injury apparently had little long-term effect. We have certainly not found any evidence that physical abuse *of itself* (except in the most exceptional and extreme cases) causes long-term harm.

Chapter 4

Current family relationships and children's outcomes

As described in chapter 1, the formerly abused children were far from a homogeneous group: some were performing well on all the measures of developmental competence while others had serious and widespread problems. In chapters 2 and 3 we looked to see whether differences in the Index children's past experiences could explain the wide variations in their current performance. We found very little association between the circumstances of the original abuse, or whether abuse was repeated, and children's outcomes at follow-up. The amount of change and disruption to children's lives also failed to explain differences in their present-day performance. Thus, on the evidence available, there seemed to be little or no direct influence of the past upon the present. This chapter will examine the effects of the children's present-day circumstances. For this exercise, we have information for the Comparison as well as the Index children. We shall therefore examine the effect of family circumstances and relationships in both groups, as well as looking to see whether the family relationships of the Index and Comparison groups differed. In the interview with the main caregiver we collected information on three factors: the caregiver's parenting style; his or her perception of family problems; and the sources of his or her social support.

The interview with the main parent figure contained a section on the approach to child rearing (*parenting style*). The main dimensions examined were:

Involvement

- Did three or more named activities with child in last month
- Does things 'regularly' with child
- 'Usually' enjoys doing things with child
- Doesn't find it difficult to spend time with child
- Had recent personal conversation with child lasting at least 5 minutes

Supervision

- Child not allowed out alone other than immediate locality or specified other places
- Has to tell parent exactly where s/he is going
- Parent knows where child is all or more of time
- Parent knows who child is with all or most of time
- Parent knows what child is doing all or most of time

Physical punishment

- Number of times either parent in the last year said they threw something at the child, pushed, shook, slapped, thumped, kicked, burned or choked child, beat him up or hit him with an implement
- Parent gave example of recent control episode where physical punishment used

Punitive style

- Number of punishment methods 'often' used: ignored/showed displeasure with child; stopped pocket money; kept in; shouted; made threats; explained why something shouldn't be done; smacked or used other physical punishment

Number of critical comments

- Parent described child as 'frequently' disobedient, arguing, fighting with siblings, in trouble with teachers, in other trouble outside home

Parent-Child difficulties

- A scale of perceived problems derived from the Family Problem Questionnaire (Gibbons et al., 1990)

From the interview with the children the following variables were extracted:

Strict

- Child described specific parental rules
- Child was sometimes afraid to tell parent the truth
- Interviewer rating of parental strictness

Good Parent/Child relationship

- Child can talk to parent about things that trouble him/her
- Parents usually keep promises
- Interviewer rating of parental dependability
- Interviewer rating of parents' positive expression

As a measure of *perceived family problems*, the main caregiver filled in the Family Problem Questionnaire (Gibbons et al., 1990) which included subscales for health, money, social contact and marital difficulties. The main caregiver also completed the Malaise Inventory (Rutter et al., 1970), containing 24 questions about emotional and physical symptoms of distress.

To measure access to sources of *social support*, the main carer was given an emended version of the Arizona Social Support Interview Schedule or ASSIS (Barrera, 1981 & 1985). Members of support networks are identified through a series of questions that probe for names of individuals who provide defined categories of social support: instrumental, emotional, and social. Informants also identify people with whom they have unpleasant disagreements. Thus the ASSIS provides an indication of conflict as well as support.

Parenting styles and children's outcomes

The seven dimensions of parenting correlated moderately with each other and also with the Parent–Child Problem Scale (Table 4.i).

Table 4.i **Correlations between parenting measures**

	Super-vision	Involve-ment	Criticism	Phys. pun.	Punitive	Strictness	Positive relat.	Parent-child probs
Supervision	1.0	.20				.22		
Involvement		1.0	−.27			.24	.34	−.33
Criticism			1.0	.40	.37			.33
Phys. Pun.				1.0	.42			.36
Punitive					1.0			.29
Strictness						1.0	.28	
Positive Rel.							1.0	−.20
Parent-child problems								1.0

Correlations with 1-tailed Significance of .001 shown

The parents' accounts of their own behaviour were corroborated to some extent by the children. Thus the child's view of parental *strictness* was positively related to the parent's account of the amount of *supervision* they exercised; and the child's view of a warmly positive relationship with the parent was related to the parent's account of their involvement with the child. From the child's point of view, parental *strictness* appeared desirable in the sense that it was positively correlated with measures of warmth and positive expression. The strongest positive correlations (though still not above 0.4) were between measures of physical punishment, punitive style and critical comments. However, only critical comments were (weakly) inversely related to the child's view of whether the relationship with the parents was a good one. The use of physical punishment and a generally punitive style, as described by the parent, did not lead the child to view the relationship as a wholly bad one.

The fact that the correlations were at a fairly moderate level suggests that the dimensions are different, though overlapping. They are not just different ways of describing the same parental behaviour.

There were few differences between lone parents and couples on these measures. Lone parents were seen as less strict by their children (p<.05) but they described themselves as more punitive (p<.05).

The next step was to see whether any of these dimensions of parental behaviour were related to the children's scores on the measures of behaviour and school performance. For this purpose we took the three factors (behaviour at home and school, cognitive test performance), the child's fears and depression scores and problems with peers.

We first examined the effect of parenting variables in the total sample (combining Index and Comparison children).

The child's behaviour problems at home

This factor was most strongly related to high levels of parental *criticism*, recent *physical punishment*, a *punitive style* and the Parent-child Problem scale. It was negatively correlated with the child's rating of a *good parental relationship*. These associations would have occurred by chance less than one in a hundred times.

The child's behaviour problems at school

This factor was significantly positively associated (p<.001) with *parental criticism* and a *punitive style*. It was negatively associated with a *good parental relationship*. In other words children whose teachers rated them as having many behaviour problems at school were more likely to be exposed to a critical, punitive parental style and to lack a warmly positive relationship with parents.

Cognitive test scores

This factor was significantly positively associated (p<.001) with the child's rating of parental *strictness* and *good relationship* and negatively associated with parental *criticism*.

Child's depression score

This factor was negatively associated (p<.001) with the child's rating of a *good parental relationship*: the more depressed the less good the relationship with parents.

Child's fears score

No significant relationships with parenting variables were found.

Problems with peers

Children exposed to more parental *criticism*, a more *punitive* style, more *recent physical punishment* and whose parents scored high on the Parent-Child Problem scale also had more problems with peers (p<.001).

Strong relationships, therefore, appeared to exist between dimensions of parenting behaviour and the child's behaviour and school performance. The relationship was strongest in the case of factor 1 – derived from the parent's description of the child's behaviour at home. This obviously raises the question of circularity – the association's being due to hostile, critical or anxious parents describing their children in excessively negative ways. However, this cannot be the sole explanation, since strong associations were also found between *teachers'* ratings and measures of parental style.

In the total sample six dimensions of parenting were significantly associated with the child's summary outcome profile – parent-child problems, criticism, punitive style, physical punishment, child's ratings of strictness and good relationship with parents (Table 4ii).

Table 4.ii **Children's outcome profiles and dimensions of parenting**

	Outcome profile			
Parenting	**Poor (79)**	**Good (89)**	**Low (89)**	**Sig.**
Parent-child problems	18.4	14.7	13.6	.0000
Criticism	1.66	0.76	0.93	.0000
Punitive	2.01	1.04	0.93	.0000
Physical punishment	1.90	0.92	1.10	.0001
Strictness	2.09	2.38	2.28	.040
Good relationship	2.29	2.77	2.52	.0001

One way analysis of variance

Did parenting dimensions operate in the same way in Index and Comparison groups?

The next step was to look separately at the relationship between parenting dimensions and children's outcome profiles in case it differed as between Index and Comparison groups. In fact there was no difference: the parenting dimensions seemed to have the same effects, for good or ill, whether the child was in the Index or Comparison group. Criticism and punitive style remained strongly associated with poor outcome in both groups. Physical punishment was more significantly associated in the Index group, but there was a strong trend in the same direction for the Comparison children; while the child's ratings of a good parental relationship were more significantly associated with outcome in the Comparison group but the trend was the same way for Index children. Thus it is tempting to conclude that these parental behaviours affected children's behaviour whether or not they had suffered physical abuse in the past.

Differences between parenting experiences of Index and Control children

The last step was to test whether Index children were more likely to experience 'harmful' parenting styles – indicated by high levels of criticism, punitiveness and use of physical punishment, and low levels of strictness and perceived good relations. As shown in chapter 1, Index children had real, though not very large, deficits in development compared to the Comparison group. Could differential exposure to 'harmful' styles of parenting in the present provide a partial explanation?

Oneway analysis of variance showed that Index children were significantly more likely to experience recent physical punishment ($p<.05$) and to be exposed to a punitive style of parenting ($p = .001$). Their caregivers reported significantly more parent-child problems ($p = .008$). There was a strong trend for Index children to receive more criticism, to have parents who were less involved with them, to be less well supervised and to rate the relationship as less good. Thus Index children did appear to be receiving a less optimum level of parenting *in the present*, quite apart from the different exposure to abuse in their early years. However, the differences were not very large and could not entirely account for the over-representation of the Index children in the poor outcome cluster.

Problems of the main caregiver

The main caregivers of the Index children had more symptoms of emotional distress, poorer health and more money problems than did the caregivers of the Comparison children, and they were less satisfied with their opportunities for social contact (Table 4.iii).

Parent ratings of children's behaviour were significantly correlated with malaise scores ($p<.001$) and with social contact problems ($p<.001$). The malaise score was also significantly associated with the children's outcome profile ($p = .0000$). Teachers' ratings of behaviour at school were significantly correlated with parents' money problems ($p<.001$). No other outcome measures showed any relationship to parents' problem scores.

We tested to see whether the over-representation of Index children in the poor outcome cluster could be explained by the fact that their caregivers were apparently more depressed. However, when malaise level was held constant

Table 4.iii **Problems of main caregiver**

Problem type	Mean score		Sig.
	Index	Comparison	
Malaise	5.67	3.59	.0000
Health	6.32	5.52	.04
Money	12.89	10.67	.0006
Social Contact	9.98	8.64	.005

One way analysis of variance

the differences in Index and Comparison children's outcome clusters remained highly significant. Therefore the differences in outcome cannot be attributed to the existence of greater parental depression in the Index group.

Relationships between adult partners

The main caregiver indicated which of a number of pre-coded 'marital' statuses best fitted his or her situation. Table 4.iv shows that there was no statistically significant difference between the Index and Comparison groups, although fewer of the Index caregivers were married or cohabiting with a partner, more had non-resident men or women friends and more had no sexual partner. (Although more Index caregivers were lone parents, many of them had ongoing relationships with sexual partners).

Surprisingly, there was also no significant difference between Index and Comparison groups in the length of time the partnerships had existed – a mean length of just over 14 years for Index and 16 years for Comparison groups. 'Resident' partnerships had lasted much longer than others in both groups.

There was a consistent tendency for the Index partnerships to contain more conflict and violence than the partnerships in the Comparison group. There had been an episode of violence in the last year in 27% of Index partnerships compared to 16% of Comparison partnerships (p = .06). The mean number of types of recent violence was higher in the Index group (p<.05). Scores on the Marital Problem scale were higher in the Index group (p<.05); and the mean number of topics mentioned as provoking rows was greater (p<.05).

The findings illustrate the high levels of domestic violence in the general population since, although the Index children were more likely to be living with warring adults, a significant minority of Comparison children was also in this situation. This violence occurred in all social classes, but the excess in

Table 4.iv **Partnership status of caregivers**

Type of partnership	Index		Comparison	
	N	**%**	**N**	**%**
Married/cohabiting	91	64	111	77
Non-resident partner staying regularly	5	3	4	3
Man/woman friend	15	11	8	6
No single friend	1	1	3	2
No partner	27	19	16	11
Other	3	2	2	1
All	142	100	144	100

Data missing on 2 cases

the Index group was more marked at the upper end of the social scale. There was domestic violence in 22% of professional and managerial families in the Index group, compared with only 10% in the Comparison group.

Effects on children's outcome

In the total sample, children in the good outcome cluster were least likely to be exposed to marital problems and recent domestic violence and children in the poor outcome cluster were most likely to be so (p<.05). The relationship between poor outcome and conflict between the adults in the household was stronger in the Index than in the Comparison group. However, adult conflict was not powerful enough to explain much of the variation in children's outcomes within or between the groups.

Social support available to the main caregiver

Supporters are people who provide 'supplies of money, materials, skills and cognitive guidance' to improve an individual's handling of difficulties in everyday life. They 'help the individual mobilise his psychological resources and master his emotional burdens' (Caplan, 1974). The people who are available to provide an individual with this help may be described, meta-phorically, as that individual's 'support system' (Gottlieb, 1983). Support flows through interactions with others. An individual's personality and social skills therefore are important in eliciting support from others, or cutting him or her off from support.

> Effective gatherers of support . . . are people who have the ability to form and sustain relationships marked by intimate exchange and by communication that penetrates beneath superficial levels. Moreover, in such relationships, people can often get support without having to ask for it. Pearlin, 1985 p. 46

People securely embedded in relationships of this kind are thus likely to have 'healthy' personalities to start with. But the existence of these supportive ties is also believed to have an important effect on mental health and well-being, through providing for the individual a feeling of belonging, reference figures and norms of conduct. In addition to these 'main effects' of support (or, according to some writers on the subject, alternatively to them) the existence of support is believed to have a 'buffering effect' in the presence of stress. When an individual is put under strain by some life change or chronic difficulty he or she will be more able to cope without succumbing to physical or mental illness if there is adequate support.

Is it possible that the parents of children who did poorly had less effective support systems? Did the parents of children who did well have stronger and more effective support systems which enabled them to cope better with the child's problems?

Size of support systems

There were few differences between the Index and Comparison carers in the overall numbers of people mentioned as ever giving support, or numbers of relatives seen in the previous four weeks, and there was also little difference in the composition of their networks although Index caregivers named a higher proportion of professionals (7% v 4%). They also named fewer confidants – a difference that was barely statistically significant at the 5% level (Table 4.v).

Subjective view of support

The Index caregivers expressed significantly more *need* for two kinds of support – confidants with whom to talk about personal feelings and people to give advice. They were significantly less *satisfied* with five of the seven different kinds of support – help with children, personal confidants, practical help (other than money or goods), advice and socialising (table 4.vi).

Index caregivers described more conflict in their networks: 20% of the relatives named were a source of conflict (15% of Comparison relatives). The greater the number of conflicted relationships the less the caregiver's satisfaction with support (p<.001). The level of parent-child problems as perceived by the parent, and the teachers' rating of problems at school, with the parental malaise score, best predicted the level of satisfaction with support. In other

Table 4.v **Number of available supporters**

	Index carer (143)	Comparison carer (144)
Relatives seen last 4 weeks	6.30	7.86
Number available to:		
Talk about personal/private feelings	2.17	2.52*
Give/lend money or goods	2.63	2.93
Give advice	1.99	2.25
Give praise/thanks etc	3.45	3.33
Help with children	2.52	2.59
Practical help in house etc	2.15	2.48
Socialise/leisure activities etc	3.70	3.97
Mean number of available supporters	10.05	10.64

* p<.05 oneway analysis of variance

Table 4.vi **Satisfaction with support**

	% Satisfied	
Type of support	Index (143)	Comparison (144)
Talk about personal feelings	76	92 ***
Give/lend money or goods	91	94
Advise	83	90 *
Praise/thank	68	72
Help with children	67	91 ***
Practical help	69	84 **
Socialise	66	74 *

* p<.05 ** p<.01 *** p<.001

words, the parents who felt dissatisfied were also the ones who identified most problems with their children, (as did their teachers at school) and in addition experienced a high level of personal emotional distress.

Among the Index carers, dissatisfaction with support was most likely among adoptive parents, and parents whose household composition had not changed since the original abuse.

Parents' support and children's outcomes

In the Index group, children whose parents had highly conflicted support networks were less likely to have good outcome profiles. The number of supporters named by the parent was only associated with the child's outcome in the Comparison group. In both Index and Comparison groups, children whose parents were satisfied with their available support had significantly better outcome profiles (Table 4.vii).

Table 4.vii **Parents' support systems and children's outcome profiles**

| | Outcome | | | | | | | |
| | Poor | | Good | | Low Performance | | Significance | |
	I	C	I	C	I	C	I	C
Mean supporters	9.1	7.7	8.1	11.5	9.9	8.8	NS	.003
Mean conflicted	1.3	0.9	0.8	0.6	0.4	0.8	.004	NS
Mean conflicted support	1.2	0.8	0.6	0.7	0.5	0.8	.02	NS
Satisfaction with support	4.6	5.3	5.3	6.1	5.6	5.9	.01	.04

I + Index, C = Comparison

Conclusion

This chapter has examined aspects of current family relationships to see how Index and Comparison children differed; and second, how current family relationships related to children's scores on the measures of development.

Certain kinds of parenting behaviour were important in relation to children's performance on these measures in both Index and Comparison groups. A set of behaviours was particularly associated with worse overall outcome: parental punitiveness, highly critical attitudes and recent physical punishment. Children who saw their parents as strict and those who described generally warm and positive relations with parents were more likely to have good overall outcomes.

Index children were experiencing significantly more of the 'harmful' punitive parenting and recent physical punishment and their parents scored significantly higher on the Parent–Child Problem Scale.

The parents of the Index children were under significantly greater stress from money worries, lack of social contacts and health problems. They scored significantly higher on the Malaise Inventory – a measure of emotional distress. Money problems and malaise scores of parents were both associated with poorer outcomes for children. Index children were more likely to be living with warring adults in households where there was domestic violence.

Finally, Index caregivers had more conflicted relationships with relatives and were less satisfied with the social support available to them. Parents' dissatisfaction with social support was significantly associated with children's outcomes in Index and Comparison groups.

We conclude that the children's experience of family relationships and styles of parenting in the present, at the time of follow-up, may have had an effect on their behaviour and educational performance; and that Index children were experiencing less optimum styles of parenting, from caregivers who were under greater stress and felt inadequately supported. Social status, poverty and lone parenthood appeared to have little independent effect on children's behaviour problems or depression but did have some effect on educational performance.

Chapter 5

The children's views of themselves and their worlds

So far, we have tried to look objectively at the children's status on measures of development nine to ten years after the experience of physical abuse, and what may have influenced it. In this chapter we shall try to gain more understanding of the children's own views of their activities, their friends and their families as expressed in their interviews.

Organised activities

Children described the extent to which they played organised games or sporting activities, went to organised clubs and had regular hobbies. They were asked how often they felt bored. Participation in organised activities (at least as described by children themselves) did not appear to discriminate in any consistent way between formerly abused and other children, nor in a clear-cut way between children with generally good school performance and behaviour and others (Table 5.i).

Table 5.i **Outcome cluster and participation in organised activities**

	Index (129)			Comparison (128)		
	Good	Poor	Low P	Good	Poor	Low P
	% regularly participating					
Sport	25	28	23	31	8	21
Hobbies	54	67	55	64	52	48
Clubs	57	44	38	47	32	50
% seldom/never bored	21	22	23	33	28	14

Friends and social relationships

Twenty questions in different parts of the interview with children were concerned with their relations with peers, since we expected that children with serious problems affecting their development would have difficulties in making and keeping friends. As discussed in chapter 1, adults did perceive a disproportionate number of the Index children as 'not liked' by others and the Index children described themselves as having more problems with peers than did the Comparison children.

Children were asked to name their friends at school, outside school or in both places. They listed the people they enjoyed playing with and the number they thought they might fall out with, and with whom they had recently quarrelled. They were asked about circumstances in which bullying had happened – whether they were the aggressors or the victims. Table 5.ii illustrates the answers.

In the Comparison sample, (but not in the Index one) there were significant differences between children in the three outcome clusters: those with good outcomes named more people who were friends both in and out of school, more people they enjoyed playing with and more close friends. They less often described themselves as being bullied or as bullying others.

While bullying usually involved some kind of physical attack or threat, sometimes it was done through name-calling and teasing. Some quotations from children who were bullied will make this clearer.

Table 5.ii **Outcome cluster and number of friends**

	Index (129)			Comparison (128)		
	Good	Poor	Low P	Good	Poor	Low P
Friends at school	2.9	3.4	2.5	2.6	1.9	2.3
Friends outside school	1.6	2.3	1.7	1.6	1.8	2.3
Friends in both places	2.5	2.1	1.8	2.9	1.7	2.3*
Enjoy playing with	4.6	4.7	4.3	4.8	3.4	3.9**
Enjoy playing with last 4 weeks	3.9	3.6	3.1	4.3	2.8	3.4**
Close friends	1.4	1.4	1.4	1.5	0.9	1.1*
Quarrel with	2.2	2.6	2.1	1.8	2.1	1.8
Quarrelled with last 4 weeks	1.8	1.7	1.2	1.1	1.2	1.1
% often/sometimes gets bullied	32	63	40	28	60	50*
% often/sometimes bullies	21	33	28	13	40	24*

one way analysis of variance *P<.05 **P<.01

> *As I'm hanging my coat up, they pull my ears and say "Hallo Bigears, where's Noddy?" When they're playing football and I'm skipping round the playground they kick the ball at me and say 'Fatso, move it". (162)*
>
> *They batter me and they all gang up on me. They get me on the floor and they keep punching me and batter me and the teacher doesn't do anything, she just doesn't care. (101)*
>
> *They start pushing me around. There's a boy who doesn't live on the street but he visits his nan. He just walks up to me and punches me in the face. I don't know why. There's a lot of people on this road who don't like me and he's one of them . . . Couple of boys down the road, they just walk up to me and ask if I want a fight, or taking things off me, calling me names, or spattering eggs on the window. (37)*

Children were reluctant to admit that they might be seen as bullies by others. For example one boy complained of being bullied in the park. When asked, 'Would you say you ever bully other kids at school or outside?' he replied,

> *Sometimes if I'm fed up. But I don't bully them like X does with me. I just play jokes. Sort of when they jog in the park and I just jump out of a tree and scare them . . . Some girls up the road shout at us. Sometimes we try and avoid it but sometimes we lift up the fence and pour water on them and they get dead mucky. I love doing that. Then their parents tell our mums and we get into trouble. (120)*

A number of friendship items distinguished between the Index and Comparison samples, regardless of the outcome cluster (Table 5.iii). The differences were not large, but all would have occurred by chance less than 1 in 100 times.

In general therefore, the formerly abused children did seem to see themselves as having less satisfying friendships and as at more risk from other children's anger. However, there was no evidence that formerly abused children who felt they had plenty of friends were likely to have significantly better outcomes. The picture was different in the Comparison group, where

Table 5.iii **Friendship items discriminating between Index and Comparison samples**

Parents don't approve of friends
Parents don't take child and friends out
Number quarrelled with last month
Number expect to quarrel with
Would like more friends
Would like to spend more time with others of own age
Friends don't visit
Gets bullied

children with poor outcome profiles also appeared to be the ones who had fewer friends. It is difficult to interpret these findings. They may be merely an artefact, due to differential establishment of rapport in the interviews. It might be that the Comparison children who were in the poor outcome cluster were more realistic about themselves and their relations with others, while the formerly abused were less able to identify whether someone was a friend or not.

Children's support systems

In their interviews, the children answered specific questions about the people they talked to about private things; the people who ever praised them or things they did; the people who would help with jobs they had to do, homework or other practical things like transport; and the people with whom they played or went on outings. They also identified the people with whom they were likely to have an unpleasant upset or row. The people identified in this way were conceived of as the members of the children's support system. Table 5.iv shows the numbers of people identified as performing the various functions. The only significant differences between Index and Comparison children were in the numbers with whom they expected to have an unpleasant upset, and the numbers with whom they had actually done so in the previous month. Just as with the parents, there was no difference in the number of available supporters.

There were no differences in the sex distribution of the people named by Index and Comparison children – just over half being male in each case – nor in the relative proportions of children and adults – with just under a quarter being adults in each case.

Table 5.iv **Number of supporters identified by children**

	Index (129)	Comparison (128)
Mean N supporters	10.4	10.1
Mean N conflicted	2.3	1.8*
Mean N conflicted last month	1.5	1.1*
Mean named friends	6.8	6.6
People to talk to about private things	2.5	2.3
People who tell you they like something you did	3.5	3.2
People to help with jobs etc	2.3	2.2
People to play with	1.6	1.5

Satisfaction with and need for support

Just as with the parents, there were differences between Index and Comparison in need for and satisfaction with support (P<.05). Index children particularly wanted more praise for things they did and more people to play or enjoy themselves with. Thus although the *quantity* of support appeared little different, from the Index children's point of view there was a difference in *quality*.

Composition of children's support systems

The differences were not large but as in the case of their parents, the Index children's networks contained a relatively higher proportion of professionals – teachers, social workers etc – and also of people identified as neither relatives nor friends. There were fewer parents, siblings and friends.

On the whole, the same functions were performed by both networks. However, there was a striking difference in relation to parents. In the Index children's networks, 14% of the parents identified were named as soruces of unpleasant upsets, but this was true of only 4% of the Comparison childrens' parents (p<.001). Thus the Index children were significantly more likely to identify their parents (but not any of the other network member groups) as sources of pain and conflict: 21 of them did so compared to only 8 of the comparison children (table 5.v).

Among the Index children, those who had been placed with 'new parents' – especially by adoption – were most likely to name a parent figure as a source of conflict.

Bad behaviour

Children were asked if they or their friends ever got into trouble with grown-ups, and then more specifically about skipping school, being expelled or suspended, and taking things that didn't belong to them. None of these items distinguished between the Index and Comparison samples, but there was an association between the child's own admission of stealing and the outcome cluster they were placed in (p<.01). 23% of all children with a poor outcome admitted to stealing, compared to 11% of low performance children and 4% of those with good outcome.

Family relationships

Siblings

Just under a quarter of children in both Index and Comparison samples had no siblings living in the same household. All those with siblings were asked how much they could count on a sibling to stick up for them, how

Table 5.v   **Members of child networks named as sources of conflict**

Relationship	% Conflicted	
	Index	Comparison
Parents	14	4.5 ***
Siblings	54	53
Friends	4	3
Other non-professional	66	56
Professionals	4	5

*** p<.001 chi sq test

much they got picked on by siblings, got blamed for things that siblings did and had fights with siblings. Overall, children with poor outcomes tended to get picked on, blamed and fight with siblings, regardless of which sample they were in. These children perhaps felt isolated even within their families.

Parents
1. Spending time together

In general, children with poor outcomes tended to mention fewer activities done jointly with mother, and described much less enjoyment of such activities (p<.01). There was no such trend in respect of father.

2. Resources

A number of questions concerned the amount of pocket money children were given, by whom, and whether they were expected to earn money. Similar proportions in both samples received no pocket money at all on a regular basis (25% v 20%). About half received less than £2 a week, and about a quarter had more than that weekly. In the Comparison sample children with a poor outcome received less pocket money, but this was not true of the Index sample. In all groups, the mother was a much more likely source of pocket money than was father alone, or both parents. Over a third of children in both samples earned some of their pocket money by domestic or other work inside the home, or by outside work.

3. Discipline

The interview attempted to establish how closely the child felt supervised by the parents; whether the child was aware of and could describe 'rules' – general guidelines about specific kinds of behaviour such as bedtime or going out alone – that were made inside the family; the child's attitude to the rules;

and what happened if the rules were broken. These aspects were measured by a mixture of interviewers' ratings of children's answers to open-ended questions, children's responses to closed questions, and their responses to analogue scales.

For example, one child in answer to the question 'Some children's parents always want to know where they are and what they are doing but other children's parents hardly ever check up on them. What about you? Are you more like the children whose parents check up on them a lot? Or are you like the ones whose parents don't often check on them?' drew a mark on the line very close to the end labelled 'Parents always want to know'. She then explained the family rules – 'If I have homework I've go to do it straight away . . . If I go out I've got to tell them where I'm going . . . Got to go to bed at 9.0 pm'. She felt these rules were fair and said there were no arguments about them. She felt "in between" about whether the rules tended to chop and change; and she was also in the middle on knowing how parents would react if she did something wrong. However, the only method of parental punishment she identified was the parent 'explaining why something was wrong'. "My mum usually does the telling off and my dad just sits there and says don't do it again".

Only two items discriminated between the Index and Comparison samples. Formerly abused children were more likely to say they were 'sometimes' or 'often' smacked or hit if they did something wrong (8% v 2% often smacked); and they were more likely to say they were frightened to tell dad (but not mum) the truth for fear of what he might do (20% v 6% often frightened).

In both samples, children with poor outcomes were more likely to see parental rules as unfair, or to be in open rebellion (Table 5.vi).

However, the great majority of children in both samples and all three outcome clusters were able to describe family rules to the interviewers, and also considered that the rules were generally fair. Only a minority, even among those with the poorest outcome, expressed disaffection.

In a further test of the predictability of discipline within the family, children were asked 'Some kids almost always know how their parents will react to something they've done, but other kids really can't tell how parents will react to something they've done. Which kids are more like you?' To answer this, children marked a scale extending from 'Always know' at one end to 'Never know' at the other end. The position of these marks was subsequently measured to give a numeric score. Children in both samples with poor outcome profiles were significantly more likely to see their parents' reactions as unpredictable (p = .01).

A similar question was asked about how clear the rules were, but this did not discriminate between the outcome clusters.

Table 5.vi **Interviewer ratings of children's statements about family rules**

	Outcome clusters		
	Good (89) %	Poor (79) %	Low performance (88) %
Rules usually fair	93	73	83
No rules elicited	3	10	9
Rules not very fair	2	7	5
Rules unfair but child complies	2	5	3
Child rebellious	0	5	0
	100	100	100

ch sq 18.0 df 8 sig .02

Children were asked about parental methods of punishment, how fair they thought punishments were, who usually told them off and whether there was a difference between mum and dad. Only methods of punishment were associated with children's outcome profiles (Table 5.vii).

In summary, there was evidence that parental styles of discipline, as perceived by children, may have had some connection with children's problem behaviour and poor academic performance. It seemed that children were less likely to do well if there were no parental rules, or the rules were not accepted by the child; if the parental response to bad behaviour was unpredictable; and if the parent's favoured methods of punishment were physical or making threats.

Table 5.vii **Methods of punishment: association with children's outcomes**

Method	Association with outcome cluster
Parents ignore, won't speak to you	No
Parents deprive you of something eg stop pocket money, keep you in	No
Parents shout/make threats	Poor outcome (P<.01)
Parents explain why something is wrong	No
Parents smack you/hit you	Poor outcome (P<.05)

4. The Reliability of Parents

Children were asked questions about how readily available their parents were to them, how much they were to be counted on and whether they kept their promises. All these questions measured aspects of how dependable and reliable this crucial relationship was, from the child's point of view.

The Index children were more likely than the Comparison ones to see their parents as very busy, and not having much time for them (P<.05). They were more likely to say their fathers did not keep their promises (P<.01).

Five items were found to be associated with children's outcome profiles. Half of those with poor outcomes (but less than a third of the rest) felt that they could not rely on mother to be there when they needed her (P<.05). Twenty-eight per cent of those with poor outcomes (compared with 8% of others) felt that they could not count on mother and that she might let them down (P<.01). Only 57% of those with poor outcomes felt that when mother made a promise she usually kept it, compared with 91% of those with good outcomes and 71% of those with low performance (P<.001). Fathers were rated as usually likely to keep their promises by 52% of those in the poor outcome cluster, 84% of those in the good outcome cluster, and 71% of those with low performance (P<.01).

Interviewer ratings of parental dependability (from the child's statements) did not discriminate between the samples or the outcome clusters. Interviewers rated mothers of poor outcome children as significantly less available to them (P<.01).

There did appear to be a considerable amount of consistent evidence that children were less likely to do well if, from their point of view, their parents could not be relied or depended upon. Some children had already, at the mean age of eleven, apparently faced the fact that they could not really trust their parents.

5. Warmth

The warmth and closeness of children's relations with their parents were tested by questions about whether children talked to parents about things that were troubling them, how much they were praised and encouraged by parents, and how parents showed children they were fond of them. Interviewers made summary ratings of the degree to which children confided in parents and the amount of positive warmth they got from parents.

For example, one child felt she could definitely talk to her mother and sometimes to her father. In answer to the question 'Some children are often praised (told nice things about themselves) by their parents, but other children hardly ever get praised. Which children are more like you?' she marked the end of the line very close to 'Often get told nice things'. She explained parents 'like my painting, my sewing and I do my make-up'. Both parents were equally likely to give praise. When asked 'How do they show they're fond of you?' she replied, 'Smile, talk cuddle . . . buy us nice things . . . They always promise to get things and do it'.

The interviewer ratings of positive warmth discriminated between the two samples and also between outcome clusters. A third of children in the poor outcome cluster were rated (from the children's statements) as receiving little positive expression of warmth from mother, compared with only 9% of those with good outcomes. Children with poor outcomes also rated themselves as less often getting praise and positive affection, but the differences were not statistically significant.

In general, children who felt their parents praised and appreciated them tended also to feel their parents had time to spend with them, that the parents kept a check on their activities and that they were fair. Being a good parent, from the child's point of view, did not seem to mean letting the child do as she or he liked, but involved exercising some control in a fair way within a relationship of concern and affection for the child. Reliability and predictability emerged as important qualities for parents to cultivate.

PART TWO

Protection and support
The effects of intervention

Chapter 6

Separation from natural parents and children's outcomes

The Children Act 1989 introduced a different framework within which local authorities and other agencies must carry out their responsibilities for child protection. Parents retain responsibility for their children, even when there is a court order (short of adoption) and local authorities must seek to work in partnership with parents, trying whenever possible to reach voluntary arrangements to safeguard children's welfare. The picture was different in the 1980s, when the protective work that is the subject of this study was carried out. Then the climate favoured 'permanency planning' – which often meant pressure to place children in permanent adoptive homes. However, the provisions of the 1989 Act are designed "to promote decisive action when necessary to protect children" (DH, 1991 p2). Since the social services department retains the lead responsibility, social workers in particular are faced with awesomely difficult decisions in seeking to strike an acceptable balance between unnecessarily heavy-handed protective action and culpably overlooking risks to a child's safety.

When practitioners turn to research seeking advice on the wisdom of separating children from abusive parents, they find no clear-cut guidelines. Elmer (1977), in an early follow-up study of physically abused young children, found that those placed in substitute families fared worse on some measures of development. Lynch & Roberts (1982) also found no advantage for physically abused children removed from their own homes. However, Hensey et al. (1983) reported significantly better outcomes for abused children who were permanently removed from their own parents.

Aim of chapter

This chapter will describe the formerly abused children's family situations nine to ten years after registration; how many had been removed to adoptive or foster homes, in what circumstances; the safety of children in different family settings; and whether children with different caregivers developed differently. The initial hypothesis was that children removed from abusive caregivers to permanent adoptive homes would have better outcomes.

Response rate

As many of the permanently separated children (42 out of 49) were interviewed as of the children who remained with one or both of their original parents (102 out of 121). Thus there was no bias from missing a larger proportion of separated children.

Change in parent figures

Just over three-quarters of the 144 formerly abused children experienced a loss of, or change in, their parent figures between the index abuse and follow-up nine to ten years later (Table 6.i).

Table 6.i **Change in caregivers 9–10 years post-registration**

	Number	%	% still with perp.
No change:			
2 Parents	24	17	79
1 Parent	11	7	73
Change:			
Lone mother, father gone	35	24	37
Lone father, mother gone	4	3	75
With mother + new father	24	17	29
With father + new mother	4	3	25
2 new parents	40	27	0
Lone new parent	1	1	0
Residential care	1	1	0
All	144	100	35

Only 17% were with the same two parents at follow-up as at the time of the index abuse, and another 7% were with the same lone parent. About three-quarters of these groups were still living with the original perpetrator of abuse (as identified in the 1981 record).

About a quarter were still with their mothers, who had become lone parents with the loss of the original male father figure. He had often been responsible for the index abuse, so only 37% of this group were still with the original perpetrator. Approaching a fifth had lost the original father figure (again often the perpetrator) but he had been replaced with a new male figure in the household. A few were still with the original father figure, having lost the mother. In three out of four cases of children with a lone father, he was the original perpetrator.

Altogether, 29% were with neither original parent. By definition, none of this group were with the original perpetrator. Of the 42 children removed from home and still in new families at the time of follow-up, 17% were fostered with a relative, 38% were fostered with a non-relative and 43% were adopted. Only one child was in residential care (figure 4).

Thus most of the abused children had to come to terms with the loss of one or both of their parents and the most commonly observed reasons for

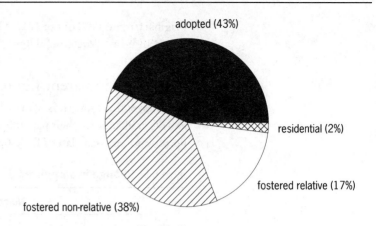

Figure 4   Type of placement at follow-up

changes were not legal actions by protective agencies, but decisions of parents to split or reconstitute their families. All but one of the children permanently removed from home (the 'separated' group) were in stable family settings, demonstrating the careful planning of the responsible social services agencies.

Baseline differences between separated and non-separated children

We compared the circumstances in 1981 of the separated and non-separated children, using the variables described in chapter 2. There were few striking differences, but four variables were found to characterise the separated group: they were living in poorer circumstances in 1981; neglectful parenting was more often mentioned in the record; the case conference more often recommended care proceedings; and the adopted children were younger at the time of the index case conference (table 6.ii).

Table 6.ii   **Baseline characteristics of children in permanent placements at follow-up**

Baseline characteristic	Adopted	Fostered	All placed	Not placed at follow-up	Sig
Months old at conference	13.8	26.8	21.1	23.8	.029
No. poverty indicators	2.2	2.5	2.4	1.7	.018
% neglect mentioned	56	60	58	28	.018
% care proceedings recommended	53	35	42.5	23	.031
Base N	18	23	41	102	

One child in residential care omitted

There were no apparent differences in the circumstances or seriousness of the abuse itself, nor in the child's previous history of abuse or of moves and changes prior to the index abuse, nor in measures of the child's physical vulnerability – birth weight, birth problems and previous illnesses. The original parents of the children in permanent placements did not have more recorded violence and criminality in 1981. On the whole, therefore, the children in foster and adoptive homes at follow-up did not differ greatly from the remaining children. However, neglectful parenting in 1981 (which as we saw in chapter 2 was associated with poorer outcome) was more prevalent in the separated group.

Circumstances of separation: adopted children

It is known that adoption is more difficult in the case of older children (Thoburn, 1990). We therefore examined the age at which the child had first been separated from the natural mother, the number of moves between different carers before adoption and the age the child was first placed in the adoptive family.

Three-quarters of the adopted group had experienced their first separation from the natural mother before the age of one year, and only two children had apparently not been separated before the age of three. On average, the children had experienced four changes of carer before the adoptive place-ment. These carer changes came about from parents' mobility and crises such as imprisonment when babies were left with friends or relatives as well as from official intervention. Table 6.iii shows the age at which the children first entered the adoptive family. Eight had joined the adopters before the age of two; eight more before the age of three; and only two between the ages of three and five. All the adopted children had been in their families for at least seven years by the time of follow-up.

Table 6.iii **Age at placement in present adoptive family**

Age (years)	N	%
Under 1	4	22.2
1 < 2	4	22.2
2 < 3	8	44.5
3 < 6	2	11.1
All	18	100

Children in long-term foster care

There were 23 children in more or less permanent foster care at the time of follow-up – seven with grandparents and 16 with unrelated carers.

These children had remained with their natural parents for longer before the first separation. Only three of the 16 with unrelated foster carers were known to have been separated before the age of one and a quarter were apparently not separated until over the age of three. However, they had experienced just as many changes of carer as the adopted children (4.4 on average). Table 6.iv illustrates the age at which the follow-up foster placement started.

Table 6.iv   Age at placement in present foster family

Age (years)	Related (7)		Unrelated (16)	
	N	%	N	%
Under 1	1	14.3	2	12.5
1 < 2	0	–	1	6.3
2 < 3	2	28.6	2	12.5
3 < 6	1	14.3	3	18.7
6 < 10	2	28.6	3	18.7
10 or more	1	14.3	3	18.7
NK	0	–	2	12.5
All	7	100.1	16	99.9

Children in long-term foster care had joined their present carers at older ages. Whereas 89% of children in adoptive homes had been placed there before the age of three, only half those with unrelated foster carers and less than half the children with grandparents had joined them before three. No child was placed for adoption over the age of five, but nine of the 21 fostered children where information was available were placed over that age. They had spent a shorter period than the adopted group in their present placements: less than half had been there for seven years.

The one child in residential care entered it at the age of six, and again at the age of nine. Because of his family's extreme mobility he was virtually lost to social services contact between the ages of two and six.

Reflecting the prevailing values in much social work with children and families in the early 1980s, there was evidence from the contemporary records that a high proportion of the natural parents (10 out of 18) had attempted to oppose adoption. The local authority had used methods such as withdrawing access and assuming parental rights and the courts had supported local authority plans. However, in five of the 18 cases the mothers had explicitly requested or agreed to adoption, often in tragic circumstances.

Outcomes of Children in Permanent Placements

Change in material circumstances

The separated children tended to come from the poorest families in the most disadvantaged circumstances in 1981 and they experienced a striking change as a result of removal from their natural parents. Nearly twice as many of the fostered and adopted as of the non-separated were in families headed by someone in a managerial, professional or clerical occupation; while three times as many of the non-separated were in families headed by unskilled or semi-skilled manual workers or people who could not be classified (Table 6.v).

Table 6.v   **Social class at follow-up: separated and non-separated children**

	Social class		
	1, 2 & 3N	**3M**	**4 & 5**
Child status	% in social class		
Non-separated (100)	23	32	45
Adopted (18)	45	44	11
Fostered (23)	48	39	13

Data missing on 3 cases

The mean disadvantage score (based on number of children, unemployment, poor housing and lack of consumer goods) was three times higher for the non-separated than for the adopted ($p < .001$). None of the adopted, only 4% of the fostered but 49% of the non-separated were living with lone parents. Children in new families, then, usually moved from socially disadvantaged to privileged circumstances. Four children also moved from black or mixed race natural parents to white adopters. Thus many children had to adapt to very different social demands and expectations.

Safety

How was children's safety affected by placement and changes in the household? Twenty-six (18%) of the follow-up sample suffered documented physical injury after registration. As we saw in chapter 3, this is a minimum estimate. Injuries were rarely serious. One child was injured in a children's home and the rest were injured at home.

Seven of these children were protected by being moved to foster or adoptive homes where they still were at the time of follow-up. No children in substitute families suffered abuse after moving there. Thus children were effectively protected by this form of official intervention.

Four children were removed temporarily after the subsequent injury but returned home, and in another five cases the father, who was the perpetrator, left the household making it unnecessary to remove the child. In one case information was not available and in eight cases the records did not indicate that any protective action had been taken. In two of these there appeared to be continuing risk and minor, unexplained injuries to the child.

The occurrence of subsequent abuse provided a partial explanation for the instability of the Index group's families and the change in parent figures. If there was subsequent abuse, children were usually safeguarded by the removal of the perpetrator, whether this was done formally through legal intervention, or by the non-abusing parent taking action to rid the household of the source of danger. This picture of prompt and effective action to prevent further repetition of abuse may have some bearing on the fact that subsequent abuse was not related to children's developmental outcomes (see chapter 3). Very few children were left at risk for long: one further episode was usually enough to trigger effective protective action.

Developmental outcomes

We first compared the performance of the separated and non-separated groups on the various outcome measures. Dr Gordon made a detailed analysis, using standard analysis of variance techniques, of the children's performance on each individual outcome measure (described in chapter 1), controlling for the child's sex, age, poverty indicators at baseline and severity of abuse.

This analysis showed that children in foster and adoptive homes, as a group, scored significantly better on four measures:

- height
- weight
- British Picture Vocabulary Scale
- Prosocial Behaviour Questionnaire

The children in substitute homes on average were physically larger and had better verbal ability. This was explained by their higher social class position. Teachers rated them as showing more positive behaviours at school. There were no differences on measures of behaviour problems at home and at school (Rutter A and B scales); no differences on other cognitive measures (Raven's

Matrices and British Ability Scales); and no differences in peer problems. There were no differences in scores on the Fears questionnaire but children in adoptive homes scored significantly higher on the Depression questionnaire.

When scores on the three factors (summarising behaviour at home, behaviour at school and cognitive performance) were compared, no significant difference could be found between children in substitute homes and the remainder. Children in adoptive homes had higher scores on the fears and depression factor.

There were no differences in the overall outcome profiles of non-separated and separated children. Twenty-one per cent of the non-separated had a good outcome – few behaviour difficulties and good cognitive performance – compared with 19% of the separated. Rushton et al., (1993), in a study of 16 permanent placements of older children, found good outcomes in seven after eight years – a rather higher proportion than in the present study, though different measures were used. Thirty-nine percent of non-separated had a poor outcome – many behaviour problems at home and school and low cognitive performance – compared with 40% of the separated. Another 39% of the non-separated were in the intermediate group, without many behaviour difficulties but with poor cognitive performance, compared with 40% of the separated.

Figure 5 illustrates the overall outcomes of the adopted children compared with the fostered and non-separated. Adopted children were more likely to

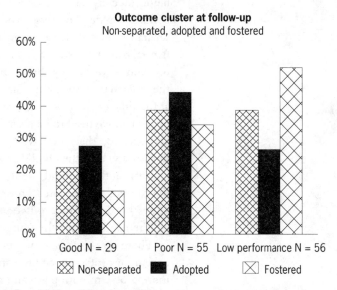

Note 1: One child in residential care with a very poor outcome excluded
Note 2: Data missing on 3 children

Figure 5 Outcome cluster at follow-up

have good or poor outcomes and less likely to be in the intermediate, low performance cluster. However, the differences were not statistically significant.

Age at placement and outcome

Children who were placed with permanent substitute carers as babies and remained with them might be expected to do better than those placed at older ages or after further serious problems in home care. However, within the separated group there was no clear trend for age at placement to be associated with good outcome. A quarter of those placed for adoption before the age of one year were in the good outcome cluster, but half were in the poor outcome cluster. In the fostered group, no child placed before the age of three was in the good outcome cluster, but three placed over that age had a good outcome. However, six of the nine children who joined their foster placement over the age of six had a poor outcome. We conclude that differing ages at placement could not explain the differences in outcome within the separated group.

Adoption and foster care: behavioural outcomes

It has been suggested by some that, as a general rule, foster care is a worse and adoption is a better alternative for children needing substitute care. As we have seen, in the sample of abused children adoption and foster care were being used in rather different ways. Adoption was used for the youngest children: a decision was made at the beginning to go for permanent separation and this was often forced through over the opposition of the natural parents. Foster care was more often used at a later stage, after a further breakdown of care by the natural parents. Foster children were older when they joined their substitute families and had been in them for a shorter period at the time of follow-up. In comparing the performance of the two types of placement we need to be clear first, that we are not comparing like with like and second, that they were not interchangeable but used for different purposes within the child care system.

Bearing this in mind, we shall now examine the behavioural outcomes of the fostered and adopted groups in more detail. Table 6.vi shows the mean scores on the separate outcome measures for the two groups of separated children and also for the non-separated.

There was a consistent trend for the adopted children to show more behaviour problems at home and school, less prosocial behaviour at school, more problems with peers and more depression compared with the children in foster care. The differences generally did not reach statistically significant levels, and there were no significant differences on the summary outcome factors. However, it is clear that the original hypothesis, that children in

Table 6.vi **Behavioural outcomes of adopted and fostered children**

Measure	Adopted (18)	Fostered (23)	Non-separated (100)
Parent behaviour rating	14.5	12.2	13.9
Parent conduct rating	3.2	2.0	2.4
Teacher behaviour rating	11.2	7.8	11.4
Teacher antisocial rating	2.9	1.7	2.6
Teacher prosocial rating	19.9	23.7	18.5
Problems with peers	2.4	1.4*	1.8
Fears score	31.2	30.4	27.0
Depression score	11.8	8.3*	9.1

Oneway analysis of variance * p<.05

permanent adoptive placements would have better outcomes, was not supported. On all the measures of behaviour children in foster care did best, with non-separated children generally in the middle.

Parenting behaviour

As described in chapter 4, measures of parenting behaviour were found to be related to children's outcomes. We shall now see whether adoptive and foster parents used different parenting methods. If foster carers were more successful in avoiding apparently harmful punitive parental styles, for example, this might provide a reason why children in foster care tended to have fewer behaviour problems.

Adoptive, foster and natural parents did differ on four dimensions of parenting (table 6.vii). Adoptive parents used most physical punishment in the last year and foster carers least, with natural parents intermediate. Adoptive parents had the most punitive style and foster carers the least. Natural and adoptive parents were most critical of their children and foster carers least. Foster carers were most involved with their children and natural parents least, with adoptive parents intermediate. Parents' critical comments, use of physical punishment and punitive style were associated with poor outcome in the total sample. Thus the children in adoptive homes appeared in some cases to be receiving a style of parenting that was not helping them towards optimum development, while children in foster care may have been benefiting from a more warmly involved and less punitive parenting style.

Table 6.vii **Differences in parenting between adoptive, foster and natural parents**

Measure	Adopted	Fostered	Natural
	mean scores		
Physical punishment	2.7	0.56	1.37***
Punitive	2.4	1.0	1.5**
Critical	1.2	0.4	1.3**
Involved	2.6	3.2	2.2***

Oneway analysis of variance ** p<.01 *** p<.001

Parents' problems

Adoptive, foster and natural parents also differed on measures of stress (table 6.viii). Adoptive parents had more money problems, more difficulties in making satisfactory social contacts and more problems with partners than foster carers. They had higher scores on the Malaise Inventory. Natural parents, however, were the most heavily stressed group as would be expected from the fact that they were much more likely to be living in poverty and coping with the difficulties of lone parenthood.

Table 6.viii **Parents' scores on measures of stress**

Problem	Adopted	Fostered	Natural
	mean scores		
Money	10.6	8.7	14.2****
Social contact	10.4	6.8	10.6***
Partner	6.4	5.2	7.6*
Malaise	5.1	3.0	6.4**

Oneway analysis of variance * p<.05 ** p<.01 *** p<.001 **** p<.0001

Discussion

The results showed that children placed on registers following physical abuse were highly likely to lose one or both natural parents in the nine to ten year follow-up period. This came about through official protective intervention to remove a child from an abusive home, but also from action by parents themselves. Mothers in particular often acted to dissolve a violent relationship and eject an abusive partner from the household. They were then about as likely to end up as lone parents in conditions of some poverty as to share their households with another man. Children who remained with their natural parents were severely materially disadvantaged in comparison with the children who were placed in substitute families.

The children in substitute families in this sample did show some advantages in physical development and verbal ability, related to the professional and managerial backgrounds of the new parents. But measures of behaviour problems at home and school failed to find any advantages for the separated group of children.

Particular advantages have been claimed for adoption as opposed to foster care. In the present study the two forms of placement had been used rather differently, with children being adopted earlier while those in foster care tended to have been removed later, after further failures of home care. Thus the foster children might be expected to have less chance of overcoming the problems resulting from early poor rearing. In fact, there was no consistent association between age at placement and children's outcomes. There was a consistent trend for the children in foster care to have fewer behaviour problems, as rated by parents and teachers, fewer problems with peers and less depression, while the adopted group tended to have higher problem scores than children who remained with natural parents. It should be noted that this result is out of line with the weight of evidence from other studies, suggesting more favourable outcomes for children in adoptive homes (Sinclair, pers. comm.).

How might the negative findings be explained? First, the follow-up point, while nine to ten years on from placement on the child protection register, still marked a relatively early stage in children's lives – they were only 11 on average. There is time for further maturation and a very different picture might be revealed after another ten years. Second, there is some evidence that around the age of 11 there may be a 'dip' in adopted children's performance for reasons that are not clear (Maughan & Pickles, 1990). If this were so, then the adopted group might come out of the dip in a further few years. Thirdly, it is possible that the adopted children differed from the remainder in some characteristics that weighed heavily against good outcome and were not captured by the study's baseline measures. There could have been pre-existing differences between the groups that were not identified because of the limitations of records. Lastly, even though a high proportion of the original sample took part in the follow-up and no more children in substitute families were 'missed', it is possible that the missing cases in some way distorted the findings.

However, the most obvious difference between the adopted and fostered groups lay in their current experiences of family life. It seemed that adoptive parents were not always using particularly sensitive methods of child-rearing.

They tended to be more punitive and to use more physical punishment and these parenting styles were associated with poor outcomes for children in the total sample. Adoptive parents also tended to have more personal problems and to be more depressed than foster carers. They were often faced with children showing difficult and disturbed behaviour but, unlike the foster carers, they rarely had professional support and advice and they felt more isolated. It is perhaps not surprising that some fell back on punitive methods.

The need for more consistent post-adoption services is being increasingly recognised (Howe, 1992; Rushton et al., 1993).

In considering these results, it is important to take into account the climate of opinion at the time most of the social work was carried out. Within social service departments there was a strong policy emphasis on planning for permanence, and this was usually interpreted to mean rapid replacement in adoptive homes if parents were assessed as inadequate carers. The majority of the adopted children in the study had been separated from natural parents who wanted to keep them by means of legal methods which are no longer available. Such a start may have influenced the subsequent course of the placement. Current adoption policy is also more aware of the need to take children's cultural backgrounds into account when planning placement, so that the very wide discrepancies in the present study would probably not be found in today's climate of professional opinion.

This chapter should not end without some recognition of the loving and patient approach of many substitute families to the damaged children in their care, although it is impossible adequately to record their work without danger to confidentiality. Some disguised examples are given in the Appendix to this chapter. The records of some children showed how improvements in behaviour and adaptation to school were slowly occurring, even though there were setbacks. However, it is important to recognise that the provision of a new family for a child who has suffered abuse is not of itself enough to improve that child's life chances. Placement creates some new problems – more changes of carer, need to adjust to changing parental demands and expectations, loss of important aspects of one's own identity. 'New' parents can rarely hope for quick returns for their love and care, and ultimate success may well depend on exceptional levels of altruism, child-rearing skills and confidence.

* * * * *

APPENDIX

Five Examples: Separated Children

Christine

Christine was born when her mother was still at school. Mother had been sexually abused by a relative and was further traumatised by the court hearing when she was accused by the man's barrister of enticing him by her provocative behaviour. On returning to school after this mother smashed up some furniture and slashed her wrists. Social Services was already involved with mother's family because of their many practical difficulties. The social worker continued to help mother, arranging a mother and baby home and later encouraging her to continue her studies by arranging a day nursery place. Mother was faced with a near-impossible task as she had no money and little support. She could not cope with the baby, who was placed on the register after a minor injury. She dreaded telling Christine of her paternity and finally requested adoption when Christine was two. The child was placed with a couple who had two older children and the Adoption Order was granted when she was three. Christine was black and the adoptive family was white.

At follow-up Christine, now aged 10, was living with the adoptive family and a younger adopted sibling. Both parents worked in professional occupations. The family lived in a large, untidy but comfortable house filled with books. Mother found the neighbourhood very friendly and felt generally satisfied with the support available though she lacked advice and opportunities to enjoy herself. She felt under considerable strain. Mother was fairly satisfied with Christine's teaching at school. She was "statemented" and had been assessed by a psychologist. She had difficulties with maths but there were no resources to give her the help she needed. She was "way behind" academically but mother expected her to get a few GCSEs and leave at 16.

The parents had been married for over 20 years but the marriage had come under pressure since the adoption of Christine. Mother felt dissatisfied with her husband, though she described him as a "very stable, secure sort of person. He's taken us all on and he'll stick with us now."

Mother described Christine as rather lacking in friends but taking part in several organised activities. She was allowed considerable freedom but had to tell mother exactly where she was going and with whom. Parents did things with her like teaching her French or going to the cinema. It was sometimes enjoyable but it was difficult to spend time with Christine because of her moods and temper. Recently Christine had got into a rage at a drama practice and then hit mother who was driving her home. Mother was extremely angry because of the danger and threatened not to take her anywhere again. Both parents were often angry with and often punished Christine but she was never smacked. Christine's difficult behaviour had driven them into family therapy and she was still seeing a child psychiatrist. However, mother felt that the child was gradually getting more control over her own behaviour and "the good things about her are getting better". She was very loving in between the upsets.

Christine told the interviewer her main interests were reading and writing poetry and going to a drama club. She had three good friends and others she played with – games like quick cricket and doctor doctor. She felt some of her friends had recently turned against her and told funny stories about her. She could count on her brothers and sisters to stick up for her. She shared a lot of activities with mother – such as swimming, tennis, and shopping – and dad helped with her music practice and took them out at weekends. There were definite family rules: "Not allowed to cook while parents are out, not allowed to go out unless you say where you're going. If someone in the family gets on your nerves don't immediately blow up but talk it over with mum or dad. If I haven't been all that nice or I show signs of being pretty tired I have to go to bed at 9.0pm but otherwise I can stay up till 10.0pm." She felt the rules were reasonable but if she ever thought they were wrong she told mum and dad so. If she did something wrong, "if it's really bad like going out without telling them then I sometimes lose my pocket money. Otherwise they just say I should know better." She was never smacked: "They've realised violence isn't the way to handle the situation, even if you feel like it". Christine felt mother was often too busy to have time for her and sometimes let her down. Mother did try to help but sometimes didn't understand – dad was better. She often got praise from parents – for example for her piano playing, or the way she handled rows with friends, or her clothes. She could talk to both about any troubles she had.

The interviewer described Christine as a very intelligent little girl who thought about all the questions and had a very good vocabulary. Christine said she had really enjoyed the interview.

Christine was rated as having a number of behaviour problems at home and at school. She often had temper tantrums and occasionally stole from home. She tended to be unpopular and get into fights. She was irritable and appeared miserable. She was fearful of new situations. Her performance on cognitive tests was rather above the average for the Index sample and she scored low on self-rated fears and depression.

Gary and John

The natural family was very well known to Social Services before the abuse incident. The children had been taken into voluntary care several times. The boys were well cared for physically and mother appeared fond of them but her own involvements with various men and her own needs took precedence. The circumstances of the injury to Gary remained obscure. Mother hinted that someone else had done it but as she was pregnant at the time they had decided she would take the blame as she expected a "lighter sentence".

After the injury when the children were between one and two they were both removed to a residential nursery under a Place of Safety Order and Social Services then obtained a care order. They were moved to a foster home and then to a family group home before joining the prospective adopters when they were between two and three. The Adoption Order was granted about a year later.

At follow-up the boys, now between 10 and 12, were living with their adoptive parents in very comfortable circumstances. Father was a company director and mother had a professional occupation. They had a beautiful house but few friends in the neighbourhood. Mother felt she needed a little more support and she was often anxious and depressed. She was in close touch with the boys' school with which she was very satisfied. She expected both to get A levels and go on to college.

The parents had been married for 14 years. Nearly all the domestic responsibility fell on her. They had disagreements which were occasionally violent. However, she was satisfied with her marriage and described husband as "generous, kind, helpful when he can be – when he's around".

The boys were closely supervised. Both parents enjoyed doing things with them but it was difficult to find the time. Mother had intimate talks with both: "I always try to make five or ten minutes before they go to bed to talk." The boys fought with each other a lot and Gary quite often got into trouble for disobedience at home and school. Both parents were quite punitive and occasionally used physical methods. Gary was forgetful and often got into trouble over not doing homework.

Gary said he regularly attended athletics club, went to cubs and pursued researches into the habits of sharks. He played football and other games with a group of friends every day – "I have the ideas. We have a vote about who wants to do what." He and his friends often fell out and then he played alone or with the girls. He got on "awfully" with his brother, who teased and wouldn't play with him. He loved going for bike rides with mum and sometimes going into work with dad. He felt parents kept a very close check on him and that there were definite rules which he usually agreed with: "You can't put your feet on the settee unless you've got no shoes on. Don't bring the hamster in. Don't bounce on your bed. Not allowed to go out without permission. Have to do your homework as soon as you come in and not watch TV until you've finished. Not allowed to watch 15 or 18 certificated films." He was sometimes smacked by mum if he did something wrong and he thought she might be too strict. He often felt frightened to tell her the truth about something he'd done. He felt both parents were too busy to have much time for him but he could count on them for help, they kept their promises and he could talk to them both about worries. He wasn't praised often but did get praised and hugged if he did something good, like playing to them on the guitar or winning an athletic event.

John also did athletics and played basketball and tennis. He collected various posters and transformers. He named seven friends with whom he played every day as well as four or five others with whom he had rows and upsets at school. His best friend once turned against him because "I think I made him kiss a girl" but basically "he and I both have the same minds". He felt he got along 75% badly with his brother. Like Gary, he felt closely supervised by parents and was clear about the family rules which he thought were "quite good". He always knew how his parents would react to his behaviour. If he did something wrong "I get told off and if it's really, really, really bad I get smacked." Mother was too strict in his opinion. He felt neither parent would ever let him down seriously. They usually kept their promises although dad had disappointed him by coming home late from work when "he had a secret with me and I was dying to know. I really couldn't wait". He was often praised and cuddled.

John had very few behaviour problems at home or school, was well above average for the Index sample on cognitive test performance and had low depression and fears scores. Gary had a few more behaviour problems at school but even better cognitive performance.

The interviewer found both boys very friendly and polite, apparently enjoying being interviewed and communicating well.

Janice

Janice's family had extensive contact with Social Services and when she was nearly two a sibling was taken into care following the discovery of bruises. Janice was first removed under a care order at this time but could not settle in foster homes and was returned home on trial. Janice may have been mistreated in a foster home at this period. The natural parents then went to court to try to recover Janice's sibling from care. At court bruises on Janice's face were noticed and she was immediately returned to foster care, now aged four. The parents were allowed supervised access but then the foster carers reported that access visits had a bad effect on Janice's behaviour. The foster father gained promotion and the family moved to another part of the country with Janice. At this point they applied to adopt her and an Order was finally granted when she was eight, at which point the case was closed.

At follow-up Janice (now in her teens) was living with the adoptive parents – both professionals – and their child who was the same age. The parents owned a four-bedroomed house in a pleasant but isolated district. Mother had a large supportive network that included Janice's natural grandparents. She felt very satisfied with her 16 year old marriage, saying of husband, "He knows me very well, he's sensitive to my moods, very understanding. Whatever he does it will be for me and the family. I trust him implicitly." There were occasional rows which included violence on her part.

Mother described Janice as having few friends and as largely inactive apart from watching TV soaps. Mother kept a close watch on Janice. She was critical of her in a number of ways, finding her poor personal hygiene particularly distressing. She had sought psychiatric help because of Janice's stealing, lying and disruptive behaviour. "We've given her so much time over the years that ⟨our own child⟩ was being neglected. We don't enjoy doing things with her – she won't let you . . . It's uncomfortable . . . You don't know what she's going to do next . . . An uneasy atmosphere." A few weeks ago Janice had run away from home for a night with a friend who was in care. This had worried them terribly. "There's just persistent aggravation from her. For our own sanity and on the advice of a psychiatrist there are certain things we ignore. She used to say at school that we didn't care for her, didn't give her anything. She was untouched by what we said." Both parents often used different forms of punishment in response to Janice's behaviour but had given up smacking her.

Mother expected Janice would leave school at 16 and thought she might do "something vocational, not academic – nursery assistant or kennel maid." Father commented Janice would probably get the same job as her mother – a prostitute's.

Janice told the interviewer she enjoyed riding her bike, looking after her dog and collecting models of animals. She named six friends but felt she needed more. She often fell out with friends and found it difficult because most lived so far away. She was very frightened of older boys at school who bullied her and other girls. Teachers knew about this but not her parents. Teachers figured largely in her support system. Janice felt she got on badly with her sibling and had problems with parents. There were a great many small rules – things Janice was supposed to do at different times of day but frequently did not. Then she had to go to bed early or miss TV for a few days. She saw parents as thoroughly predictable and reliable. She was often frightened to tell parents the truth. She could not tell either of them of her worries. She wasn't often praised – "Because I don't do anything out of school it's not possible for them to praise me."

Janice had many behaviour problems at home and was rated by her teacher as having as many emotional as antisocial behaviour difficulties at school. She was well below average for the Index sample in performance on the cognitive tests and scored high on the depression questionnaire. Janice checked the items which said that most of the time I feel like crying, running away, I get tummy ache, feel that life isn't worth living, I never enjoy things as much as I used to, have horrible dreams, feel very lonely and feel so bad I can hardly stand it.

The interviewer felt this was a very sad situation, likely to get worse, and that a breakdown was foreseeable.

Robert

Robert's natural mother became pregnant with him at an early age after leaving care. She left Robert's father when she became pregnant again. Mother worked as a prostitute and was several times arrested. Her risky life style meant that Robert was frequently left with different carers. At one stage Social Services took him into care under a Place of Safety Order but he was quite soon re-united with mother, orders were allowed to lapse and they were put on a bus to a different town. Here mother continued her way of life, leaving her two children to be cared for by different people while she continued to work as a prostitute. This stage came to an end when she was arrested and imprisoned. The friend caring for the children sought help from Social Services who took the children into voluntary care. At this point bruises were found on Robert's back. He was placed on the register, Social Services assumed parental rights over the children and moved Robert and his sibling to prospective adopters when he was two. Mother would not agree to the adoption which finally went ahead when Robert was five. He was of mixed parentage and the adopters were white.

At follow-up Robert, 10, lived with the adopters and two siblings in a comfortable house that they owned. Father was self-employed. There were no money worries. Mother felt under strain and needed more support. She was fairly satisfied with the school, where she had recently contacted the headmaster over Robert's difficult behaviour. She expected him to leave at 16 and doubted whether he would have any qualifications.

The parents had been married for 17 years. There were seldom disagreements and mother felt satisfied, describing husband as "very kind, thoughtful, soft-hearted".

Mother said Robert had no organised activities and no real friends. He was "very, very close" to his natural brother. It was difficult for them to do things with Robert because "he can't sit still. He flits about from one thing to another. And he does cause arguments. Without you really realising what he's doing, he winds everyone up". He often behaved badly at home and outside. For instance, the previous night he kicked his brother and then denied it. "It doesn't matter what I do to him, he'll deny it and deny it and that's what causes the most trouble". Discipline was punitive and included frequent physical punishment. Robert thought parents were "picking on him all the time and it's only him we tell off and the whole world's against him". Mother felt she was rapidly reaching the end of her tether and complained that from the day of the adoption they had had no help whatsoever from the authorities. She felt her marriage was being stretched to the limit because of Robert's "uncontrollable" behaviour.

Robert told the interviewer he was in the school football team and enjoyed several active sports. He named several friends but wanted more. He had recently moved to a new school which was some distance away. He was bullied at school by people calling him names and working him up. He also got into trouble for throwing stones at children who called him names in the street. He got on badly with his brother and sister, did not enjoy doing things with mother but liked helping dad. He took notice of parental rules though he thought they were unfair. If he did something wrong he was grounded or got the slipper from mum. He thought both parents were busy and often not available to him. They sometimes let him down and didn't keep promises. He thought he could talk to them about worries and said he often got praise.

The interviewer commented that Robert's manner was flat and he did not seem happy but otherwise appeared a very ordinary boy.

Robert was rated by mother and teacher as having a great many behaviour problems, predominantly of a conduct disorder type. He was below average in performance on cognitive tests. He scored low on self-rated depression and fears.

Ian and Asif

The case of Ian and Asif illustrates the complexity that could characterise foster care. Their natural mother had spent most of her childhood in care and was regarded as backward. Ian first came to official notice at the age of eight months when the putative father complained to Social Services that mother was not looking after him properly. Ian was taken into voluntary care. A Supervision Order was then granted and he returned to mother after two months. After a period with her in homeless accommodation they were rehoused but Ian was found to have bruises and the remains of a burn. Mother's explanations of an accident were accepted but concerns over his care continued. When he was approaching two he was again received into voluntary care during mother's confinement for the birth of Asif. A few months later he was back home and bruises on his face were being investigated. He was found a full-time day nursery place. Further facial bruising the following year was medically diagnosed as due to a dog bite. There were three more investigations for bruises and burns found on Ian and Asif, his younger brother. All were considered accidental, the result of lack of supervision. When Ian was aged three and Asif one, Social Services obtained care orders on them both. They remained home on trial.

The following year mother moved to another area. After a period of homelessness, she and her new cohabitee were rehoused with the children to a council house. The registrations of the boys were transferred and the new area undertook supervision under the care order. When Ian was five severe healing burns were noted on him for which mother had not sought medical attention. Following a case conference both Ian and Asif were removed to foster parents.

Later the same year mother had a little girl (Julie) who was registered at birth. At this case conference it was decided to plan for long-term care for Ian and rehabilitation home for Asif. Parents now tried to get the care orders revoked with the help of the law centre. Social Services reacted by deciding to start adoption proceedings for Asif on the grounds that mother did not visit the foster home regularly. At the court hearing on revocation of the orders, however, parents and their solicitor failed to turn up, parents later claiming they had been unaware of the date. Parents were informed that their access to Ian and Asif would be stopped. At the same time Julie's name was removed from the register as there were no concerns about her care. Mother and her partner have since had two more children whose care has never been questioned.

Not long afterwards Ian's disturbed behaviour, which included bed-wetting and tantrums, and the foster mother's reaction to it began to cause concern. He was moved to a children's home to prepare for adoption. Mother and her co-habitee were now prepared to let Ian go but were determined to fight for Asif.

Ian was moved to foster parents with a view to adoption when he was 10. He soon began to display difficult and disturbed behaviour. Asif meanwhile was still with the original foster parents who now applied to adopt him. Their attitude changed when Asif too started to behave in a disturbed fashion and they requested his removal. He was sent to a children's home. Quite soon it was decided to close this home for financial reasons. At this point Ian's foster mother requested to have Asif as well. Asif moved in when he was 10 and Ian was nearly 12.

The new foster family persevered with the difficult and antisocial behaviour of both boys. They did not pursue plans for adoption as they feared being left without support from Social Services. They were receiving a high level of contact from a fostering specialist.

At follow-up Ian and Asif (now aged 14 and 12) were living with these foster parents – Ian had been with them for five years and Asif for two. Three adult foster siblings were also part of the household. Both parents had professional qualifications and the family lived in very comfortable circumstances. Ian and Asif had part-Asian origins but the other family members were white. Ian and Asif attended the local school and mother was fairly satisfied with the teaching. She expected them to leave at 16 and hopefully get training for manual or "creative" jobs. She said Ian himself wanted to be an astronaut.

Mother had plenty of friends as well as working part-time. She felt pretty satisfied with the support available to her. Her network included a named social worker on whom she relied for advice. She had been married for 27 years. It was a traditional marriage where she was responsible for household tasks while husband managed the money and domestic repairs. They seldom disagreed and she was very satisfied with her marriage, describing husband as "appreciative", "honest", "hard-working and thoughtful".

Mother told the interviewer that both children had suffered from living in an institution. They had no sense of value – they just 'lost' clothes they were bought, having no sense of possession. They had little sense of time. She felt both boys were operating at a level some three years behind their actual ages. She described Ian as popular, often visiting and being visited by friends as well as taking part in organised sports. Ian was allowed to go for long bike rides and into the city with friends but was supposed to tell parents exactly where he was going and with whom. Asif was slightly more restricted. Mother said she "would not impose her will on clothes and wouldn't really insist on bedtimes". It was "a bit of a penance" trying to find activities that she could do with the boys, partly because the parents were so busy, but she said both were able to confide in her – recently Ian and she had discussed his first girlfriend and Asif had talked to her about worries at school. Both tended to get into trouble frequently with teachers. Ian had recently shocked them by stealing some money from husband's wallet in order to buy a ring for a girl. This had almost been a relief as she had worried he might have stolen the ring. They dealt with it by withdrawing pocket money and making him do jobs at a certain rate to pay the money back. Father took the lead in discipline which was not punitive and mainly relied on explaining why certain things were wrong.

Both boys described a good many activities and friends. Asif, however, said that he was sometimes bullied at school "because I cause trouble and they remember it". At primary school he had bullied others because he was the strongest. The boys did not get on with each other (though mother felt their behaviour with each other was improving). Neither did much with their parents beyond practical jobs around the house. Ian felt parents gave him quite a bit of freedom but there were house rules he thought were fair. Asif felt more closely supervised and was more rebellious. If they did something wrong they both said they got sent to their bedrooms and told to think about it for 10 minutes when mum or dad would come up and talk about why they did it and why it was wrong. Neither was ever smacked. Both felt that parents were strict enough but not too strict, though they were sometimes frightened to tell them the truth. Both boys felt they could rely on parents. Ian said he never talked to them about his feelings but Asif could do so. Ian didn't think he got much praise but "sometimes" got a hug. Asif felt he was often praised and got a kiss every night.

The interviewer found both boys quite easy to interview. Both thought about the questions but understood them and could also handle the self-completion questionnaires. Ian in particular came over as a pleasant young man with a good sense of humour who tried hard to give honest answers.

Ian was rated as having a few behaviour difficulties at home and rather more at school. His performance on cognitive testing was about average for the Index group. He scored rather above average on self-rated depression and fears. Asif had very few behaviour problems at home or school. His performance on cognitive testing was average and he scored low on self-rated depression.

Chapter 7

Protective services and children's outcomes

Information about the services received by children and their carers came from the records of the responsible agencies. We attempted to trace all records relating to the child held by the 'key' agency (the one to which the key worker appointed by the case conference belonged). Caroline Bell carried out the bulk of the arduous task of visiting agencies and abstracting data onto standard forms. Table 7.i shows that full records for the whole follow–up period were obtained for 72% of cases, partial records for 21%, while all files had been lost, destroyed or were withheld in 7%.

Table 7.i **Accessing key agency records**

| | Number of cases | | | | | |
| | City | | County | | All | |
Documentation	N	%	N	%	N	%
Complete	57	76	66	69.5	123	72
Partial	13	17	22	23	35	21
None	5	7	7	7.5	12	7
Total	75	100	95	100	170	100
Mean data sources	2.1		1.6		1.8	

New Data Source: New key agency or new geographic area

We examined in detail the services provided during a standard 5 year follow-up period from the date of the abuse investigation in 1981. Where service had continued beyond 5 years, we abstracted information but did not analyse it in the same detailed way.

We attempted to characterise the service along the following dimensions:

Length – For how long a period in total was the case allocated to a social worker; for how long was the child on the child protection register; what was the last month of contact in the standard 5 year follow-up.

Amount of contact – During the standard 5 year follow-up, in how many months did contact between social worker and child or family take place; how many face-to-face and phone contacts were there.

Intensity of contact – How many contacts per allocated month.

Continuity – How many gaps in contact occurred during the standard 5 years (a gap being a 3 month's break in contact); how many different workers were allocated; how many different areas or agencies were involved.

Quantity and range of service – What family support services were offered; what referrals were made for other professional services (such as child psychiatry); how much contact did the social worker have with other agencies.

Structure – What social work methods were recorded as being used; were there signs of planning and organisation in the way the work was recorded (with initial summaries, plans, progress and final summaries).

Legal protection – What legal orders were made in respect of the child.

In general, social workers were allocated to these children for very long periods – far longer than the time the child remained on the register. There was a huge amount of direct contact, usually in the form of home visits. Considering the length of allocation, and the high proportion of children who moved, there was remarkable continuity, with a third of children having the same, or only two, workers throughout the follow-up period. Most families received several supportive services, money or other material help being the most common, but referral for professional treatment was less common. Formal social work methods – such as counselling, family therapy or groupwork – were rarely used. Social workers did not usually record formal assessments of the child's problems and needs and the goals they were working towards, but kept track of their work by means of progress summaries from time to time.

The typical picture was of a conscientious social worker going to great lengths to keep in regular contact with both child and carer over a long period of time, monitoring the child's welfare and helping in practical ways in the frequent marital, financial and housing crises that beset many of the families. The typical social worker remained in regular contact with a wide array of other agencies, such as nurseries, schools, health visitors, social security and housing officials, but seldom arranged professional treatment or therapy for child or carers.

The amount of contact between social workers and family and the use of legal services were related to characteristics of the child and family at the time of abuse. The amount of contact and the use of legal orders were significantly greater when the injury was more serious, neglect was mentioned, the child had been previously separated from parents and there was a larger number of poverty indicators. Children with birth problems or defects also received more social work contact.

There were marked differences between the patterns of services for non-separated, adopted and fostered children (table 7.ii). When children were in foster care the case remained open for significantly longer and there were

Table 7.ii **Key agency services by whether in substitute family at follow-up**

	Family status		
	Non-separated	**Adopted**	**Fostered**
Characteristics of service	**(102)**	**(18)**	**(23)**
Length			
Months allocated	47.8	49.0	94.0***
Months on register	33.7	31.9	29.7
Amount of contact			
Months in wh. contact	25.3	30.1	38.9***
N face-to-face	73.2	94.3	103.9
N phone	15.1	30.1	27.9**
Intensity			
Contacts per month	2.8	3.2	2.7
Continuity			
N periods	1.8	1.0	1.8**
N workers	3.1	2.9	3.5
N areas/agencies	1.7	1.5	1.8
Quantity			
N support services	4.9	4.2	3.7*
N professional refs.	0.9	0.8	0.8
N social worker/agency contact	46.2	35.0	32.1
% legal order	51.5	100	85.7***

One child in residential care omitted. Some data missing on 15 cases. *** $p<.001$
** $p<.01$ * $p<.05$

more contact months. In adopted and fostered children social work contacts were more likely to be by phone. Non-separated children received most family support services and fostered children least. Legal orders were least likely to be used for non-separated children. Since there were clear differences in the pattern of services, it is necessary to examine the relationship between services received and children's outcomes separately, *within* the non-separated, adopted and fostered groups.

Social work contact and children's outcomes

We shall start by looking to see whether the length or amount of social work contact, its continuity or its intensity had any relationship to children's overall outcomes. For the children in foster care at follow-up, there were no associations. For the non-separated and adopted children, there were trends but in opposite directions. The adopted children were more likely to be in the good outcome cluster if the case had been allocated to a social worker for a *shorter* period (p<.05); if there were *fewer* contacts with a social worker (p<.05); and fewer social work contacts with other agencies (p<.05). In other words, for adoptive cases the greater the degree of social work contact, the less good the child's overall outcome. This negative association is not likely to be a causal one, but merely reflects the seriousness of the child's problems. However, for the non-separated group, the trend was in the other direction. Non-separated children were more likely to be in the good outcome cluster if there had been *more* social work contacts (p=.10), of *greater* intensity (p=<.10), and with *fewer* gaps (p=.10). For them, there was a tendency for greater social work input to be associated with better outcome.

Social work methods

We looked to see whether the use of specific social work methods was associated with children's outcomes. To be counted, there had to be a description in the record of the deliberate use of one or more of the following methods: marital counselling, family therapy, play therapy, task-centred casework, groupwork, counselling, behavioural methods. A category 'other specified method' was used more liberally to include, for example, any mention of making agreements or contracts with parents or children or working towards definite goals. Specific social work methods were most likely to be used when children were in foster care, but they were rarely used in any group.

'Other' methods in the separated group most often involved direct work with children, especially the use of life story books. There were no significant

Table 7.iii **Social work methods**

Social work method	Non-separated	Adopted	Fostered
		% method used	
Marital counselling	7	0	0
Family therapy	2	0	10
Play therapy	4	0	15
Task-centred	0	0	0
Groupwork	1	0	5
Counselling	6	6	15
Behavioural	6	6	15
Other	26	41	50

associations between the use of any of the specific social work methods and children's outcomes. However, in the non-separated group there was a trend for the few cases where behavioural methods had been systematically used to have better outcomes (p<.10).

Family support services

Data was collected from the records about the use of nine different kinds of family support service in the five years after registration. They were: NSPCC Special Unit, other voluntary agency support, family centre, family aide, special child-minding, day nursery, voluntary reception into care (accommodation), money or material help and subsidised holiday. Figure 6 illustrates the use of family support services for non-separated, adopted and fostered children. Material help and attendance at day nurseries were the most commonly available supportive services. Material help was usually given in the form of small sums of money to pay for food or other necessaries at times of crises, or goods such as prams, bedding or fires. Although the individual sums were usually small they were often provided at intervals over several years, again illustrating how near the financial edge many of the children in non-separated families were.

There was no association between children's outcomes and the number of different family support services provided in the five years after registration.

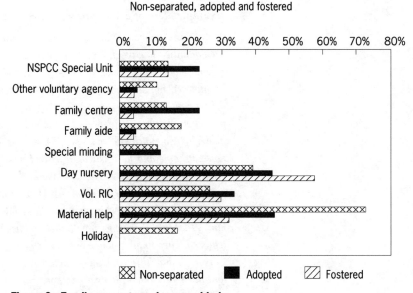

Family support services
Non-separated, adopted and fostered

Figure 6 Family support services provided

In the fostered and adopted groups, there was no association between any form of family support and children's outcomes. But in the non-separated group two forms of family support did have significant associations with good outcome. Sixty-two per cent of the children in families who received support from a voluntary agency had a good outcome compared with 18% of those in families who never received such support (p<.05). Half the children who attended family centres had a good outcome, compared with 19% of those who never attended (p<.05). Thus non-separated children whose families were linked with a family centre or with a voluntary family agency (such as Home-Start or Family Service Units) appeared to have better outcomes in the longer term, although the numbers are very small.

There appeared to be a common pattern to the cases where a good outcome had followed from links to a family centre or voluntary help. There had usually been active co-ordination from a social worker who was also unusual in that s/he often used structured social work methods focused on particular difficulties. The social worker had usually mobilised other specialist services (such as psychological) in addition to the voluntary agency. There were also legal orders (usually Supervision Orders) in three-quarters of the cases. The family centre or volunteer link may not have been the crucial factor in itself, but it represented part of a planned and purposeful approach to the problems of the child and family. The family centre in these cases was being used therapeutically, as part of a package of services, and not as a mere prelude to the child's legal removal from home. Because of the legal order the family acquired greater priority in the allocation of scarce resources.

Example: Use of a Voluntary Agency

Mother first approached the social services department for financial help after father had been admitted to a psychiatric hospital for assessment. While off sick from work he had become violent and smashed all the crockery in the house. Mother was left with no income. A month later mother brought Derek, aged two, to the social services department with bruises on his face inflicted by father. Derek was placed on the child protection register. A few weeks later mother informed the social worker that father had held a lighted match to Derek's face. Derek was not allowed to speak or make any sort of noise at home and for this reason he had hardly any language. The couple separated briefly but soon reunited. The social worker maintained intensive contact focused on the many practical and marital problems. When Derek was three a Home-Start volunteer was introduced to support mother and the social worker obtained a day nursery place for him. After further violence from father, mother had to take Derek and his siblings to a refuge. Father finally moved out – not before assaulting both mother and the social worker – and this time the separation proved permanent. Mother and children continued to receive intensive support from the social worker and the Home-Start volunteer, focused on boosting her self-confidence and ability to manage her affairs.

Derek by now was attending nursery school. When he was nearly five mother set up house with a man friend she had met at the child minder's. He had been left with two children by his wife. As the situation seemed quite stable and Derek was no longer on the register, the case was closed. The social worker had maintained regular contact for over three years.

At follow-up Derek, now 10, was living with mother and stepfather and his natural and step-siblings. Stepfather was employed in a manual job and the family lived in a house they owned with which mother was very satisfied. She felt this second marriage was a happy and secure one. There were no particular problems with Derek (although his younger sibling was very difficult). Discipline was fairly permissive and they did not use physical punishment. She had recently told Derek how proud she was of him and how she relied on him to set an example to sibling.

Derek had very few behavioural problems at home or school, scored above average on cognitive tests and had few self-rated fears or depressive symptoms.

Professional help

Information on referrals for professional help in the five years after registration was taken from the records. In the non-separated group, 26% of parents had been referred for some professional help (outside the social services department), compared with 17% in the adopted group and only 5% in the fostered group. Siblings had received professional help in 18% of non-separated cases, 17% of adopted and 5% of fostered. A quarter of the non-separated children themselves had received professional help, compared with 22% of the adopted and 48% of the fostered. Figure 7 shows the kinds of professional referral that were made. Children were most likely to be referred for specialist medical and psychiatric assessment and treatment, and parents also were most likely to be referred to adult psychiatrists.

There were no significant associations between children's outcomes and the number of different professional services used, nor any individual service. However, there was a clear trend in all three groups for referral of parent figures to adult psychiatrists or psychologists to be associated with better outcomes of children in the longer term. It may be that parents who received some psychiatric help or assessment after the original abusive incident were enabled to give better care to the children, or to come to terms more easily with placement in substitute families.

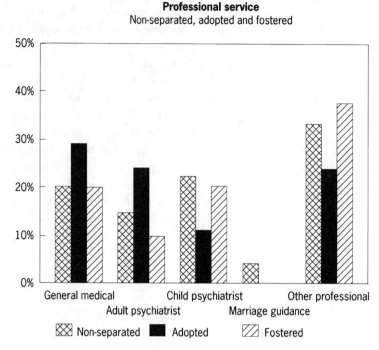

Figure 7   **Professional services provided**

Legal orders

Was there any evidence that children who remained with a natural parent under some form of legal protection did better than those who were not legally protected?

Table 7.iv shows the use of different legal orders among children who were still with a natural parent at follow-up. Neither the use of any legal order, nor

Table 7.iv   **Use of legal orders: non-separated children**

Order	% used
Place of Safety Order	
At baseline	31
Later	5
Interim Care Order	19
Supervision Order	
At baseline	25
Later	6
Care Order	11
At least 1 Legal Order	51

of a particular order, was associated with the children's outcome cluster. Thus there was no evidence that children with legal protection had better overall outcomes in the longer term. By the time of follow-up 96% of children still with a natural parent were not under any legal order, 2% were home under a Care Order and 2% were under Supervision or other orders.

Substitute care

Did children who received respite care, or those who spent longer periods away from home before being reunited with a parent, show any gains? For this purpose two groups will be considered separately:

1. Rehabilitated (Home on Trial, or returned home after at least 6 months in voluntary care).

2. In care for one or more short periods totalling less than 6 months.

Table 7.v shows the outcome for children who spent at least six months away from home, and who were all at home at the time of the follow-up assessment. Thirty-one per cent were in the good outcome cluster, rather more than in the sample as a whole. The numbers are very small, but there is a suggestion that children who went home after the age of three did better than those who were rehabilitated under that age.

Table 7.v **Outcomes of children rehabilitated from care**

Age at rehabilitation	N	% Good outcome
Under 1	1	0
1–2	5	0
3–5	6	67
6–9	1	0
All	13	31

Thirty-one children had one or more short periods in care, totalling less than six months, during the follow-up period. Nineteen per cent of these were in the good outcome cluster.

In summary, children who had been removed from natural parents for longer periods – at least six months – and then rehabilitated when they were over the age of three appeared to have somewhat better outcomes than children who had one or more shorter periods in care. However the numbers are small and no statistically significant results were found.

To sum up, the general pattern of services delivered by the key agency in the five years after registration was characterised by conscientious monitoring over several years supplemented by practical help at times of crises. There were substantial differences in services received by children in permanent substitute homes and children still with their own parents. There was some evidence that more intensive and prolonged social work contact was of benefit to children who remained with their own parents. When families were linked to voluntary agency support or to a family centre there was clear evidence of benefit. There was a trend for children whose parents had been referred to an adult psychiatrist to show better outcomes. There was no evidence that other forms of family support or professional help had any effect on children's outcomes. Children who remained with their own parents did not show significant gains from legal protection nor from periods of respite care.

Contact with social agencies at the time of follow–up

Parents were asked during their interviews about their contacts with a number of health and social agencies during the last year. We compared responses of adopted, foster and natural Index parents with those of Comparison parents (figure 8).

There was no difference in the amount of contact with general practitioners and health visitors. All three groups of Index parents were significantly more likely to have had a recent contact with the social services

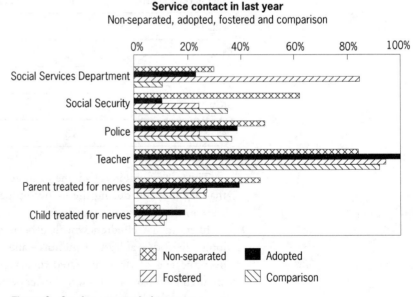

Figure 8   Service contact in last year

department than were the Comparison parents. Within the Index group foster carers, not surprisingly, reported much higher rates of contact but nearly a quarter of adoptive, and nearly a third of the non-separated parents were still in contact, compared with only 11% of Comparison parents.

Non-separated Index parents were most likely to be in recent contact with Social Security (62%), consistent with the finding of their greater exposure to social disadvantage. Comparison parents were more likely to have had a recent contact with Social Security than were adoptive or foster parents – again reflecting differences in social class status. Recent contacts with the police were quite likely in all groups, but were highest among the non-separated Index parents. The great majority of all groups had had at least one contact with their child's teacher in the last year, but the non-separated Index parents stood out from the other three groups in having a larger minority with no teacher contact.

High proportions of parents in all groups reported that they had had some treatment for 'nerves' in the last year – from general practitioners, psychiatrists or psychologists – but non-separated and adoptive parents were most likely to have had such treatment. Adopted children were about twice as likely to have had recent treatment for 'nerves' as all other groups. This is consistent with their higher scores on the Depression Questionnaire.

In summary, the evidence of recent contact with helping agencies is consistent with direct evidence from the measures of children's outcome in showing that the adopted Index children, although better off in material circumstances, were more likely to be struggling with behavioural problems and symptoms of personal distress, while the non-separated Index children were more likely to be left in poverty and material disadvantage.

PART THREE

Context and methods of the study

Chapter 8

Context of the study: a review of the literature

This review of the literature is divided into the following three main sections:

1. The effects of abuse upon a child's development.
2. The nature and effect of intervention in the lives of abusing families.
3. Life events and the abused child.

I: THE EFFECTS OF ABUSE UPON A CHILD'S DEVELOPMENT

This section reviews the numerous follow-up studies of physically abused children. Particular attention is paid to studies which have considered those areas examined in the current study, and there is also a consideration of other relevant issues namely risk and protective factors and methodology.

Methodological issues

To appreciate any review of the literature on follow-up studies of physically abused children it is first necessary to realise the methodological problems which have dogged them. Methodological problems can be broken down into the following areas:

(i)   sample size

(ii)   unrepresentative sample

(iii) comparison group

(iv) baseline, intervention and outcome data

(v)   statistical analysis

(vi) varied follow-up periods

(vii) comparability

These factors account for the questionable reliability of individual projects and the difficulty of making comparisons between them.

Sample size

The larger the sample size the more representative the sample will be of the population from which it is drawn. Also as sample size increases within-group comparisons become more feasible. However, given a situation of finite resources, as sample size increases the number of variables which can be incorporated into the research design decreases. In practice then, researchers have to reach a compromise between sample size and the number of variables.

Unfortunately follow-up studies of physically abused children tend to fall short in terms of both sample size and the number of variables studied.

Two of the most frequently quoted follow-up studies of physically abused children – Elmer (1967) and Lynch and Roberts (1982) – used samples of 11 and 42 abused children respectively. The largest sample amongst the studies reviewed was 53 (Calam and Franchi, 1987). In one of the most recently published studies only 22 children were followed-up (Wodarski et al., 1990).

In any discussions of methodological weaknesses in follow-up studies of abused children it is important to bear in mind that these weaknesses do not occur in isolation and tend to have knock-on effects. Many studies, for example, have high attrition rates – an issue which is discussed below. A high attrition rate, in conjunction with a small sample size invariably makes the sample even less representative. Given the general diversity within abused populations – a point which is discussed in more detail in the section on variables – within-group comparisons are particularly important.

Wodarski et al. (1990), for example, conducted a cross-tabulation analysis of teacher ratings of behavioural adjustment by age and sex. Four groups were produced: younger girls; older girls; younger boys; older boys. On the basis of this analysis the authors make important statements such as: 'The socio-emotional adjustment of physically abused children appears to become more problematic with age'. However, although specific figures for the size of the different groups are not given, the total sample size from which they were drawn was only 22, which means there would on average be only 5 to 6 children in each group.

Lynch and Roberts (1982) divided their sample of 42 abused children into three groups for the purposes of examining the effect of placement upon outcome. Those children where rehabilitation was attempted after a period of separation had the worst outcome. The children who were at home all the time had the best outcome. There was an intermediate outcome group consisting of children who initially went home after discharge from hospital but were then placed elsewhere. The issue of substitute care and the particular findings of this study do not come up with the appropriate confidence and reliability because the numbers in each group must be so small.

A major cause of bias in sample derives from the source of the sample. Elmer (1967) drew her sample from the Childrens' Hospital of Pittsburgh. The children in the Lynch and Roberts (1982) study were referred to the Park Hospital for residential treatment along with their families. Such samples are likely to be over-represented by more severe injury cases.

In the Lynch and Roberts (1982) sample 23 (56%) and 17 (44%) were rated severely and moderately injured. It is probable that the outcome for more severely injured children is worse than that for less severely injured children, so studies using hospital or clinic samples may tend to overstate the effect of abuse. In terms of cognitive performance alone such children will perform less well. Caffey (1972) suggests that most of the children exhibiting neurological abnormalities but with no known history of head trauma were probably subject to severe shaking. In the follow-up by Martin et al. (1974) most of the low IQ scores were explained by head trauma and neurological dysfunction.

More recently more use has been made of samples drawn from child protection agencies – Calam and Franchi (1987), Gregory and Beveridge (1984) – and children referred to social service agencies (Wodarski et al., 1990). As these groups have not excluded individuals on account of factors such as severity of injury or referral to hospital, they should be more representative of abused children as a whole. However, once the source of the sample has been identified workers may introduce selection criteria which then reduce the representativeness of the group. Gregory and Beveridge used only those children and families referred to the Special Unit of the child protection agency. This then excluded the more serious cases who, the authors themselves state, would have been subject to alternative placements, whereas the least serious cases would not have received the services of the specialist unit. Nakou et al. (1982) excluded families who had only one child.

Even after the source of a sample has been identified and the selection criteria determined the sample may still be subject to bias. A major reason for this is attrition – either through an inability to trace subjects or a refusal by subjects to take part in the research. Lynch and Roberts (1982) was one of the more successful attempts to locate and trace families for a follow-up. Of a target group of 41, 40 were traced and 39 agreed to participate. However the authors describe the exercise as the researchers' nightmare (Lynch, 1978). Several studies have encountered very serious attrition rates: Oates et al. (1984) attempted to follow-up 56 children who had been physically abused, neglected or at-risk. Only 39 of these children took part, representing an attrition rate of approximately 30%. Martin et al. (1974) managed to follow-up only 58 of an original group of 159.

Some authors have argued, Oates et al. (1984), that as the social character-istics of the lost subjects were similar to those of the sample as a whole, there is no need to be concerned at sample bias. While this point is of some validity it still does not remove the possibility that the refusers and participants are different in other ways – ways which have an important bearing upon outcome.

Wodarski et al. (1990) comment upon the nature of the refusers in their study:

> non-participation by a family may have reflected more severe abuse or
> pathology; thus the loss of such families to the study may have resulted

in underestimates of the social, emotional, academic and functional deficits in physically abused children.

Martin et al. (1974) noted that those who refused to participate in the research tended to be those who refused to accept social work intervention. Such a sub-group is of particular interest in terms of intervention both for the fact that they receive *less* intervention and also because of their attitude to intervention. Exclusion of such families from an outcome study may seriously bias the results of a study.

> The findings of the present study lead us to believe that abused children with minimal or no intervention will have a much poorer prognosis than children, such as those in our sample (Martin et al., 1974).

The bias amongst non-traced and refusing families is evidenced in other forms of research such as that from the field of delinquency where it has been shown that lost subjects are over-represented by non-white, low socio-economic status, and officially delinquent persons (Wolfgang et al., 1987).

There exists a second level of bias, in that even when families are available for research the very phenomenon under study – abuse – removes some children from the research and creates bias in the data for others.

Abused children may have been so traumatised and subject to so much intervention that those responsible for the child eg social service departments, substitute caregivers and wardship judges refuse to give permission for access, in case the research should further distress the child.

A further source of lost subjects comes in terms of specific measuring exercises. Rodeheffer and Martin (1976) identify five types of behaviour exhibited by abused children during the course of their participation in research:

1. distractibility

2. extreme manipulation

3. resistance and rebelliousness

4. elective withholding of speech

5. passive denial.

Such behaviour may well have an influence upon the child's eventual test scores. Lynch and Roberts (1982) used the Rodeheffer and Martin scheme and concluded:

> Such behaviour may not have affected the child's final attainment in the assessment but it certainly influenced his approach to the tests, his interaction with the therapist and often his enjoyment of the assessment.

Gray and Kempe (1976) found that in a research setting three quarters of an abused sample were overly-compliant and submissive while the remaining quarter exhibited acting out behaviour. Such findings are important not only in terms of research procedure but also because, if they are true of other situations eg classroom and peer-relationships, then they may have quite negative consequences for the child. As Lynch and Roberts (1982) note

> In several cases it was obviously the children's social and emotional problems that were restricting their academic potential.

It is likely that such behaviour would have some effect upon formal test results, although this has yet to be borne out. Ten children in the Elmer study failed to respond to the Columbia Mental Maturity Scale and were then given the Picture-Vocabulary subtest of the Stanford Binet Intelligence Scale or the Weschler Intelligence Scale for Children (WISC).

Other sources of bias may occur in terms of samples being over-represented by middle class children eg Lynch and Roberts (1982) and also because of how the study is explained to informants. Elmer (1967) explains that:

> The families were told that the purpose of the study was to improve hospital services; abuse and other sensitive topics were never brought up.

In the Wodarski et al. (1990) study a similar line was followed where the study was presented as:

> a study of child development and school performance.

Many studies simply do not report how the work was explained to parents, although in studies such as Lynch and Roberts (1982), where families were receiving residential therapy for abuse, then the family would have been clear about the purposes of the work.

Respondents in different studies may be given contrasting explanations as to the purposes of the study. Teachers in the Gregory and Beveridge study (1984) knew of the child's abuse history.

Comparison group

The purpose of a comparison group is to provide the researcher with a frame of reference within which the performance of the index group may be assessed. If index and comparison groups have similar distributions in terms of age, sex, social class etc. then the effect of these variables upon the dependent variables is controlled for.

Some follow-up studies have mistakenly referred to their comparison groups as control groups. Control groups are used in an experimental context where the index group is subject to the intervention and the control is not. It would be impossible to use such a research design in studies of child abuse, so the comparison group method has to be used. In particular this group is of value in that it allows instruments to be calibrated. Whereas the control group method allows causation to be speculated upon with some confidence this is not the case with the comparison group. This is especially relevant in terms of child abuse where little is known either about types of outcome or which of the numerous factors in many abused children's lives are truly significant.

This confusion between the purposes of control and comparison groups may then lead to a misinterpretation of findings, particularly in the direction of assuming too much confidence.

Some studies have simply not used comparison groups (Egeland et al., 1983). Where comparison groups have been used basic characteristics such as age, socioeconomic status and sex have not always been controlled for (Gregory and Beveridge, 1984; Wodarski, 1990). This means that differences between the index and comparison group may be explained by age, sex etc. rather than abuse or any other aspect of the abused child's life.

Other studies have drawn comparison groups from sources which raise a variety of methodological questions. Lynch and Roberts (1982) compared abused children with their siblings. While this is valuable in terms of controlling for social class and home environment it makes comparisons of age and sex problematic and makes no allowance for the fact that being raised in an abusing environment may be as serious for a child's development as being abused (Jaffe et al., 1986). In addition such a sample may contain cases of non-detected abuse.

A similar criticism may be made of Elmer (1967), who drew a comparison group from the same hospital as the index group. The comparison group had likewise suffered multiple bone injuries, raising the possibility that some of these cases were caused by physical abuse (Lamphear, 1985).

Lamphear (1986) emphasises this point saying follow-up studies need to invest more effort into ensuring the comparison group does not contain abused cases. The author goes as far as recommending observational studies such as those undertaken by Egeland and Sroufe (1981) to ensure the absence of maltreatment in the comparison group. Other authors have identified comparison groups as one of the most formidable methodological problems facing follow-up studies (Oates et al., 1984).

When comparison groups have been used it is very rare for any attempt to be made to check whether any individuals in the group have been subject to abuse. While some studies inadvertently increase the risk of including maltreated comparison children, very few studies make formal checks to ensure that any comparison child has not come to the notice of child protection agencies, Wodarski et al. (1990) being one of the few exceptions.

Baseline, intervention and outcome data

Follow-up studies of abused children face a bewilderingly complex task in attempting to unravel the role of individual variables and the interaction between variables. Within a group of physically abused children the nature of the assault, the context in which it took place and the characteristics of the victims may vary enormously. In addition the children may have been subject to other types of adversity such as neglect, witnessing violence between caregivers and hospitalisation. On top of this the children may have experienced a great deal of change and disturbance in their lives: moving home; changing school; changes in the care giving situation; separation from siblings. These factors are not confined to the baseline period but may extend well into, and beyond, the time of intervention.

Intervention may have an equally significant effect upon the life of the abused child and his/her family. The child may be removed temporarily or permanently; the family may receive intensive social work support for several years; referrals may be made to specialist therapeutic units; parents may be prosecuted; additional health visiting resources may be applied. The type, intensity and duration of intervention, and equally importantly the family's response to it, will vary considerably. In terms of outcome, abuse may affect a child's cognitive functions, education attainment, behavioural adjustment, peer relationships, emotional adjustment and language.

It can be seen therefore that an abused child may experience a wide array of factors through both his/her domestic situation and the intervention which could influence outcome. Child protection research is unfortunately not even at the stage of having reliably and comprehensively recorded these factors, let alone begun to assess the importance of different factors in terms of outcome. This is borne out by a review of follow-up studies which shows that rarely is any attempt made to break down physical abuse into basic components eg severity of injury, method of injury, relationship of perpetrator to child, nor do they record baseline and intervention data. Consequently little or no attempt has been made to examine the separate influences of aspects of the abuse or the many other factors in the life of the abused child. It is interesting to note, however, that studies into the effects of child sexual abuse have investigated basic elements of the sexual assault, such as the type of sexual act, the relationship of the victim to the perpetrator, the frequency and the duration of the abuse (Bagley, 1990; Finklehor, 1984).

Baseline data

It has been pointed out numerous times that physical abuse should not be seen in the restricted terms of just a physical assault (Oates et al., 1984; Lynch and Roberts, 1982):

> Clearly the effects of abuse are negative; however there is no direct relationship between abuse and specific developmental outcomes. This

is not surprising given the pattern, severity, frequency and intention of the actual abuse. In addition there are significant differences in the home environment of abused children which may account for the diverse developmental outcomes (Egeland and Sroufe, 1983, p460).

It is necessary therefore that any analysis of the longer term effect of both abuse and intervention should gather comprehensive data on the abuse incident and the context in which the physical assault takes place.

There are in fact a number of levels on which abuse needs to be considered. The first of these, discussed above, is the nature of the abusive act itself. The second concerns abuse as an indicator of the child-care giver relationship:

> Some researchers suggest that physical abuse is characterised more by the **chronic** use of excessive physical control tactics and ineffective child management skills than by isolated incidents of abuse . . . the effect of maltreatment on children may have more to do with the day-to-day aversive parent child interactions than the actual abusive episodes (Lamphear, 1986).

Oates et al. (1984), raising doubts about the wisdom of leaving some abused children in their own homes emphasise the importance of the general environment over and above the abuse:

> It is unlikely that it was the abusive incident itself which has caused the continuing problems [in the children]; rather the cause is likely to be the disturbed family environment which led to the abuse and in which the children have remained (p634).

It can be seen therefore that to understand the effects of abuse, data on the incident itself, parent-child relationship and the wider home environment must be provided. As other reviews have noted, (Toro, 1982; Augoustinos, 1987), these data are not adequately covered in most follow-up studies. Studies such as Kinard (1980), which looked at the intervening effect of a range of family background measures eg family structure, care giving arrangement and socioeconomic status, are rare.

Many of the studies reviewed here were not able to consider the separate and combined effect of sexual abuse in the lives of physically abused children. This is a crucial point as there is thought to be a considerable overlap in populations of physically abused and sexually abused children. Furthermore sexual abuse is thought to have profound effects upon the development of at least some children, effects which continue into adult life (Adams-Tucker, 1982; Fromuth, 1986).

What follow-up studies have recorded and to some extent analysed is the presence of neglect and emotional abuse of the physically abused child (Wodarski, 1990; Lynch and Roberts, 1982; Allen and Oliver, 1982; Speight, 1979). Many of these studies have postulated that both neglect and emotional abuse have a greater effect than physical abuse either alone or in conjunction with physical abuse.

> parental rejection and emotional abuse . . . producing long-term consequences far more devastating than those following physical abuse alone (Lynch and Roberts, 1982).

As Allen and Oliver (1982) note, the sequel attributed to the original abuse may actually be due to undetected continuing abuse. Some studies have controlled for other forms of abuse or neglect while others have not. Even amongst those which have, rarely is there any attempt to provide a definition or criteria by which the family situation was deemed to be neglectful or emotionally abusive. This leads to difficulties in verifying the validity of these labels; identifying what are the crucial elements of neglect/emotional abuse in terms of outcome, and making comparisons between studies. Usually the only definition or criteria provided is that the child has been officially labelled as neglected/emotionally abused by a child care professional (Wodarski, 1990; Nakou et al, 1982).

Creighton and Noyes (1989) have shown that physically abused children are more likely to experience a wide range of adversities as compared to the general population. The children's family life is more likely to be characterised by marital problems, unemployment, low income and geographical mobility. The negative effect of such factors on children's development is well-established but follow-up studies have rarely recorded the presence of these factors and even more rarely have they controlled for them.

Some attempts have been made to consider other adversities and life events. Elmer et al. (1967) postulated that some of the poor outcome in children was due to prematurity, maternal deprivation and child care practices in addition to the abuse. Gregory and Beveridge (1984) gathered data from register files on children. This included data on separations between caregivers; violence between caregivers; homelessness; care giver's psychiatric treatment and learning difficulty; abuse of caregivers as children and birth complications. The authors found that children from more stable home environments had better outcomes in terms of educational achievement and social adjustment. Martin et al. (1974) looked at home stability as an intervening variable in the long-term development of abused children. This was a global measure consisting of excessive disorganisation; frequent unemployment; high geographical mobility; poor management and chaotic social structure. A within-group comparison showed that abused children from unstable homes had lower IQ scores than abused children from stable homes.

Lynch and Roberts (1982) recorded higher rates than normal of both prematurity and small-for-date babies in their sample of abused children. Such factors may be important not only in explaining the context in which abuse occurred but may also be a major contributing factor, over and above that of abuse, for physical development.

Baseline data are also of importance in determining the degree of change in factors between the baseline point and the follow-up point. This is relevant in terms of evaluating the effect of intervention in areas such as parent-child relationship or home stability. Similarly in estimating a child's degree of progress it is vital to have knowledge of his/her starting point. Outcome cannot be assessed in isolation but must be related back to earlier situations. A child may score lower on a measure at follow-up but actually have made greater improvements on say growth or IQ than another child.

A further need for a full assessment of baseline and subsequent of a child's life stems from intervention studies. To appreciate the relationship between specific interventions – say in terms of placement – and outcomes, it is necessary to analyse which factors actually lay behind the placement. For example, children who are permanently removed from home against those who remain may come from quite different home situations and have experienced quite different abuse. This might have an influence on outcome, which would be lost if children were considered solely in terms of placement.

Outcome measures

Methodological problems connected with outcome measures include: validity; reliability; comparability; range and number.

Many studies have looked at only a small number and narrow range of outcome measures; language development (Allen and Oliver, 1982); social adjustment and education attainment (Gregory and Beveridge, 1984); peer group interaction (Jacobson and Straker, 1982). Aber and Cichetti (1984) have urged researchers to view the maltreated child as a whole child by considering a broader range of developmental subsystems and environmental settings.

A second problem arises in terms of cause and effect. A number of workers have suggested that the 'outcomes' being attributed to abuse may well have been present before the abuse and may in fact even have contributed to or caused it. Martin et al. (1974) and Lynch and Roberts (1982) have both suggested that some children may be at greater risk of abuse because of congenital abnormalities and ante-natal complications. These problems may have a causal relationship to later deficits. Likewise Oates et al. (1985) have suggested that their findings of fewer friends, less play, lower aspirations and expectations for abused children may have been character traits the children possessed prior to abuse and which increased their risk of being abused.

A third difficulty arises in terms of the reliability of outcome measures. While instruments of well-proven validity and reliability have been used eg Rutter's Behaviour Questionnaires, the Bristol Social Adjustment Guide, British Ability Scales, abused children may have problems eg in the sphere of emotional or behavioural adjustment, which cause interference with the variable being measured (Rodeheffer and Martin, 1979; Lynch and Roberts, 1982). It could be then that the deviancy of abused children on measures such as cognitive ability and education attainment is exaggerated.

However some studies have introduced their own methodological problems into the outcome data in terms of validity and reliability. Elmer (1967) for example 'determined the most representative IQ score for each child on the basis of these data and our tests', which consisted of intelligence test results, achievement test results, grades in particular subjects, placement in school and teachers' judgements. In the Gregory and Beveridge (1984) study teachers were asked to rate social adjustment on the BSAG, but as the authors note, the teachers were likely to have known of the child's abused status and this may have affected their perception. Lynch and Roberts (1982) estimated the children's IQ primarily by means of observation. Elmer (1967) and Lynch and Roberts (1982) also used different tests to measure a given variable for children of different age groups.

Areas such as cognitive ability, educational attainment and behaviour are sometimes routinely looked at regardless of the child's characteristics or without reference to these. However there is considerable support for looking at effects in terms of a child's age. This appears to be generally taken as the age at follow-up but it would appear to be reasonable to take into account age at abuse, and indeed age at intervention. It might be for example that a child's attachment abilities are affected at 1 year but not 10 years or that removal from home is more disturbing for a 5 year old than a 15 year old.

> Thus there is merit in placing children in developmentally relevant age groups in order to assess the effects of family distress and violence . . . research should focus on the specific stage-salient competencies eg parental attachment that may be affected by the maltreatment experience (Lamphear, 1986).

A good deal of professional child protection work is actually concerned directly with the parents, yet in terms of outcome it is the child who is the major source of attention. While the child is obviously the main cause for concern, this disparity between intervention and outcome is puzzling and disappointing.

It is important to develop more outcome measures pertaining to relevant aspects of family life eg care giver relationships; material conditions in home; stability etc.

Another crucial issue in terms of outcome is interpretation. This point is perhaps best exemplified by reference to those studies which have produced positive findings eg Calam and Franchi (1987) whose study identified abused girls performing better than a comparison group in terms of reading and arithmetic. This was explained as follows:

> The child must be at far lower risk of abuse sitting quietly reading a book than running around, splashing paint onto paper and clothes or otherwise creating noise and disturbance. Further it is possible that high achievement may enhance parental estimation. Hence, by doing well at school and by having sufficient resources to present a good face, these children may have created for themselves a safer environment.

The possibility of positive outcomes has also been shown by Martin et al. (1974). Such findings illustrate the difficulty of establishing the effects of abuse. Not only might the effects be in a direction which according to theoretical concepts is wholly unexpected but a range of interpretations may be placed upon any given finding. As Oates et al. (1984) have warned excessive parental expectations may impair children's emotional adjustment. Martin et al. (1974) noted that while extreme parental involvement may result in high academic achievement for the child, it might also lead to a decrease in the child's ability to approach problems with flexibility and imagination.

Physical development

Elmer (1967) followed up 31 children referred to the Children's Hospital of Pittsburgh. 11 of the children were deemed to have been physically abused, 12 were diagnosed as non-abused cases and the remaining 8 were unclassified. The children's health at follow-up was assessed in combined terms of height, weight and a clinical judgment of nutritional status. Elmer concluded that a large proportion of children from all three groups were, in terms of physical development, in 'surprisingly good condition'. There was a small number of both abused and non-abused children below the third centile for height and weight. Paediatric examinations showed that most of the children, in the whole sample, had organ systems in a generally good state. While Elmer's work suggests that abused children's longer-term physical development may not be very dissimilar to that of non-abused children from the same socioeconomic background, the small numbers of children in the sample and the absence of basic data such as age distribution and length of follow-up casts some doubt on the reliability and precise meaning of the data.

The study also found that at the time of admission to hospital the abused children had a higher rate of growth failure than the non-abused children. This means that many of the abused children had made a significant recovery over the follow-up period in terms of physical development. This led Elmer to reject the idea that:

> Pronounced growth failure may, under certain conditions not yet fully spelled out, cause permanent retardation of growth potential.

Although the sample size was very small, it is interesting to note that the greatest improvement in physical development was shown by children who had been removed from their homes and placed in substitute homes – either residential care or foster care. This led Elmer to state that:

> In sum, the data . . . strongly suggest that the normal growth potential of most of these abused children could be realised only when their environment was decidely improved for a prolonged period of time. Such improvement appeared to balance out both prematurity and early growth failure as influences on physical development.

In the study by Lynch and Roberts (1982) growth failure at follow-up was defined by any one of the following criteria: if the child's height or weight remained below the third centile; if it fell below the third centile, or if the yearly growth velocity (height or weight) was below the third centile. Lynch and Roberts also looked at head circumference. Again, falling below the third percentile was taken as evidence of poor physical development. There were three such children amongst the group of 42 abused children. All three of these children were diagnosed as neurologically handicapped. The inter-relationship between measures from different spheres – in this case physical and neurological – is a common theme in follow-up studies of abused children as shown in the following statement by Lynch and Roberts:

> As in Martin's study, microcephaly in our sample was associated with poor neurological and intellectual prognosis.

It may be then that while only a very small proportion of physically abused children exhibit poor physical development at follow-up, those that do may have quite severe problems.

Oates et al. (1984) followed up 39 children 5½ years after they had been officially identified as either abused, neglected or at risk. The mean age of the children at follow-up was 8.9 years. The work by Oates et al. is perhaps one of the more rigorously designed studies incorporating, for example, a comparison group of children of the same age, sex, ethnic group, social class and school. The results of this work confirmed the findings of Elmer (1967) and Lynch and Roberts (1982) in that there were no significant differences in height or weight between the abused group and the non-abused comparison group.

Cognitive Ability

Cognitive ability is one of the areas most frequently measured in follow-up studies of physically abused children. Where abused children score lower than the comparison group or lower than normal scores, these differences do not always approach significant levels. However, as was discussed in the preceding section the studies reviewed used such different methodology that comparisons are not very meaningful.

Martin et al. (1974) were able to test only 58 children from an original sample of 159 children who had been drawn from two hospitals and a child protection agency. Children completed either the WISC or the WPPSI. IQ scores were not significantly different from the normal distribution. Although scores tended to be somewhat lower than normal this was primarily accounted for by those children who had experienced head trauma or neurological dysfunction.

Oates et al. (1984) obtained results at some variance to those quoted above. Using the verbal scale and WISC-R it was found that abused children's scores were significantly worse than those of a comparison group matched on age, sex, ethnicity, social class and school. Furthermore, the authors noted that differences still remained even after the scores of neurologically damaged children had been excluded and after allowance for the standard error of measurement. This study, like the previous one quoted above, suffered a high attrition rate (30%), but in addition studied abused children the vast majority of whom were still in their original homes, which would tend to suggest that the study was under-represented by children from more disturbed homes, if not more severely abused.

The study by Lynch and Roberts (1982) found little difference between abused children and their non-abused siblings in terms of overall IQ score. However a more detailed analysis of the test results showed that in terms of non-verbal IQ both groups scored slightly higher than the normal mean. On verbal IQ both groups scored lower than the normal mean, although the differences were statistically significant only for the abused group.

Elmer (1967) identified 'mental retardation' in 45% of those children in the sample who attended school. This finding, for a sub-sample made up as it was of abused, unclassified and non-abused children, would suggest poor cognitive outcome in both abused and accidentally-injured children. In view of the small numbers involved (N=19), the over-representation of severely injured children and the range of tests used (Picture Vocabulary subtest of the Standford Binet Intelligence Scale; the Columbia Mental Maturity Scale; the Form L-M of the Stanford Binet Intelligence Scale; the WISC, and the Rorschach) the reliability of these results must be questionable. A further weakness in the methodology was that the children's IQ score was in fact based upon an estimate by research staff who 'determined the most representative IQ score for each child on the basis of these data and our tests'. Besides the tests 'these data' consisted of achievement test results, grades in particular subjects, placement in school and teacher judgments. Comparison with findings from other studies and replication is not feasible. Interestingly the practice of estimating IQ rather than relying solely upon standardised testing has been used elsewhere (Morse et al., 1970).

While these and other studies tend to suggest a small effect upon cognitive ability, little attempt is made to distinguish between abused children. Some abused children are shown to perform normally or above average on cognitive tests yet seldom are explanations put forward to account for these within-group differences, including whether or not protective factors may play a role.

Educational attainment

Wodarski et al. (1990) followed up a group of maltreated children whose age at follow-up ranged between 8 and 16 years. The sample included a total of 22 physically abused children. In addition to the small sample size it has to be noted that the follow-up was a maximum of 18 months since abuse. This might mean that any findings could be as much a product of the intensive initial intervention and the associated family instability, as the longer-term effect of abuse. In other respects, however, the Wodarski et al. study appears to have had a rigorous research design. A composite Index of overall school performance was produced. This consisted of test scores on the language and mathematics portions of the norm- and criterion-referenced Iowa Test of Basic Skills, reading scores from the Georgia Criterion Reference Test, final grades in language and mathematics, and absences for the previous year, plus the teacher assessment from the Child Behaviour Checklist. The legitimacy of combining these various measures is questionable but with this proviso in mind it is interesting to note that the abused children scored significantly worse than a fairly similar comparison group.

In terms of individual measures the abused children were significantly, after controlling for SES, worse in maths, working below par and learning below par. A sub-sample of neglected children were significantly worse than the non-maltreated group on all these measures plus reading and language. This finding of an outcome for neglected children worse than abused children has been found in a number of follow-up studies and was discussed in the previous section. A further qualification for the Wodarski et al. (1990) study is the degree of missing data. School record data – from which the majority of measures were obtained – were missing for 32% of the abused and 21% of the neglected children.

Calam and Franchi (1987) found no clear differences between an abused group (N=53) and comparison group on the school attainment section of the

Bristol Social Adjustment Guide. Indeed the abused girls acutally performed better than the comparison girls in mathematics and reading. This seemingly paradoxical finding is not unique to this study and the subject of positive outcomes for abused children is discussed in the preceding section. It is worth noting that while the Calam and Franchi sample stood to be fairly representative, being drawn as it was from a child protection register, only children referred to a child protection special unit were followed up. This study excluded children not living at home and those attending special schools. The exclusion of these groups biases the sample, probably in the direction of underestimating differences between abused and comparison children.

The lists of a child protection agency were also used to identify the sample of children in the follow-up study by Gregory and Beveridge (1984). The sample was not as representative as it could have been as it included only those children referred to the agency's Special Unit. This produced a sample which could be thought of as intermediate in terms of seriousness, with cases generating sufficient concern for referral to the specialist unit, but not being so serious as to necessitate the child's removal from home. The reliability of the study is also suspect on the grounds of sample size (N=13), comparison group selection and the means of testing the child. The majority of tets were from the British Ability Scales (BAS), in particular Word Reading, Basic Number Skills, Naming Vocabulary and Word Definition. Other tests of reading, arithmetic and comprehension were also used. Relative to the Comparison group the Index group had lower mean scores on virtually all these measures, although the difference reach significant levels only on BAS-Word Reading. On sentence comprehension and subtraction the abused group's mean was higher than that of the Comparison group. These findings, based upon children aged between 5 years 11 months and 6 years 11 months at follow-up and all abused prior to their 4th birthday, lead the authors to conclude:

> In practical terms this means that 10 of the 13 abused children had made real progress in learning to read before they were 7 years old, and that 8 of them could add and substract numbers up to 10 (p528).

The follow-up by Gregory and Beveridge was relatively short. Although the authors do not provide any baseline data there is a suggestion that abused children can progress or catch up in terms of educational attainment. This idea of 'recovery', through some mechanism, over time for abused children has been put forward by Wodarski et al. (1990) in attempting to explain the absence of socioemotional difficulties in older neglected children. This goes against those who argue that abused children's lives rendered them susceptible to cumulative deficits:

One conclusion from these findings is that the negative effects of different patterns of maltreatment on the development of the child during the first years of life are cumulative (Egeland et al., 1982, p.)

Oates et al. (1984) obtained a similar result to the Gregory and Beveridge (1984) study in terms of reading. Using the Schonell Reading Test it was shown that both abused and comparison mean scores were lower than the norm, only the abused group's score reached statistical significance. Lynch and Roberts (1982) found that 44% of their sample were below average in reading, with 41% below average in arithmetic.

As with virtually all aspects of a child's development follow-up studies taken together do not present a wholly consistent picture. Having said this it seems to be the case that abused children's educational attainment is lower than comparison children's, even after controlling for social class. Whether attainment in general is at risk or whether particular areas eg reading, are vulnerable, is unclear. There is also doubt over whether abuse has a direct effect upon attainment or whether its effect is mediated through a third factor such as language (Lynch and Roberts, 1982) or whether both abuse and poor attainment are both related to a third variable such as poor verbal stimulation at home (Oates et al., 1984).

Behaviour at school

It is in the area of behaviour at school that follow-up studies have produced the most consistent and reliable findings. This is partly a result of common methodology, in particular the frequent use of either the Rutter 'B' Scale or the Bristol Social Adjustment Guide (BSAG). Both these instruments ask teachers to rate children's socioemotional types of behaviour in the school setting.

Lynch and Roberts (1982) used both the Rutter 'B' Scale and the BSAG. There were no significant differences between the abused group and the sibling comparison group but both groups' rate of maladjustment on each instrument was much higher than in the general population. This applied to both boys and girls.

Stott (1974) advises that rather than look at the BSAG overall score, the sub-scores relating to under-reaction and over-reaction should be analysed separately. Lynch and Roberts found that in terms of under-reaction, (withdrawn, depressed, unforthcoming), there was practically no difference between the sample and the general population. This means the deviant overall score was being produced by over-reaction, forms of behaviour such as hostility, inconsequential behaviour and an inability to get on with classmates. Broken down by sex it was shown that boys and girls in the sample had the same rate of disturbed behaviour, which suggests that abused girls are equally at risk in this area, contrary to what would be expected from the contrasting rates for boys and girls found in the general population. The absence of differences between the abused group and the sibling comparison group seems to support the view of Jaffe et al. (1986), that children who witness violence in the home are as much at risk from long-term effects as children who are actually abused. While there are definite advantages to using non-abused siblings as the source of the comparison group, this latter finding is one of a number of reasons for not using this method.

The BSAG was also used by Calam and Franchi (1987) in their follow-up study. As in the Lynch and Roberts (1982) study 'over-reaction' types of behaviour were distinctive. However, unlike the previously quoted work there were 'clear and disturbing' differences between the abused and comparison group. There was also a marked difference between abused boys and girls with problem-behaviour being exhibited by 45% and 21% respectively of children in each of these groups.

Oates et al. (1984) found that abused children scored worse than a closely matched comparison group on both the anti-social and the neurotic sub-scales of the Rutter 'B' Scale. The rates were 34% v 13% for anti-social behaviour and 16% v 3% for neurotic behaviour.

This quite consistent finding of higher rates of disturbed behaviour amongst abused children, particularly for boys and possibly to a lesser, but still significant level, for girls is important in a number of respects. In terms of research it may create problems in testing children reliably, as has been encountered in a number of studies: Elmer (1967), Rodeheffer and Martin (1976), Lynch and Roberts (1982). It also means that caution has to be exercised in attributing causal relationships between variables with a high correlation. It may be, for example, that abuse does not have a direct relationship upon poor educational attainment but is mediated through a third variable of behavioural disturbance. This inter-relationship between variables was noted by Lynch and Roberts (1982):

> In several cases it was obviously the children's social and emotional problems that were restricting their academic potential (p110).

Disturbed behaviour may then have implications for the child's development in general. Academic progress, peer relationships and relationship with adults who care for the children may all suffer:

> Despite the limitations of our small numbers, the implications . . . are clear: children from abusing families can very quickly grow into difficult and disturbed individuals, disliked by their peers and frustrating and antagonising adults who try to care for them (Lynch and Roberts, 1982, p112).

Behavioural disturbance may be very pervasive and manifest itself beyond a child's school years into young adulthood. West and Farrington (1973) found that a teacher rating of troublesomeness at age of 8 years was the single best predictor of a child subsequently going on to become a juvenile delinquent.

The work of Gregory and Beveridge (1984) confirms the earlier results of children scoring higher on both the overall and the under-reaction scores of the Bristol Social Adjustment Guide. Considering the instrument in more details the authors note that the largest component in the over-reaction dimension is the inconsequence score, which was defined by Stott (1974) as:

> A failure to inhibit the first response-impulses which come into a child's mind. These are of a primitive physical type, such as aggressive responses to frustration . . . The child acts impulsively without advanced mental rehearsal of the consequences so that trials and errors take place in actual dealings with objects . . . Because his behaviour causes him to be rejected, he may develop defences in the form of antisocial and hostile attitudes.

Such character traits could have a major bearing upon a child's transition into adult life not only in areas such as delinquency but more generally in their ability to plan their lives. Indeed Gregory and Beveridge (1984) go as far to speculate on the implications this finding may have for future parenting:

> it is possible to appreciate that the inconsequential behaviour of children may have some similarities to those of the abusing parent (p530)

Conversely, it has been shown that many abused children do not show these sorts of developmental problems.

> Both Roberts et al. (1978) and Gregory and Beveridge (1984) make one point clear, however: a good percentage of children in both samples were showing satisfactory adjustment; half of Roberts' . . . sample were exhibiting no problems at all (Calam and Franchi, p24)

Calam and Franchi suggest that these seemingly good outcomes may be a product of the child behaving well to avoid further abuse or alternatively the child may be reacting in a more proactive manner by performing well at school in order to enhance parental estimation. Martin et al. (1974) have argued that the better than expected IQ scores for abused children at follow-up may indicate the existence of skills and competencies developed by the child in order to protect him/herself in a dangerous environment. These skills and competencies leading to an increase in the child's cognitive ability. While an average or above average outcome for some abused children seems well-proven, the explanation is not very well understood. Furthermore it may be that attempts by the child, such as those just described, to influence parent-child interaction may have negative consequences such as a decrease in a child's ability to play imaginatively (Martin et al., 1974; Lynch and Roberts, 1982). Following on from the findings for behavioural adjustment at school, there is some dispute as to whether teachers are best-equipped to assist the child (Lynch and Roberts, 1982) or whether the schools are unable to overcome children's behavioural problems (Oates et al., 1984).

II: INTERVENTIONS FOLLOWING ABUSE

Introduction

The literature on evaluations of interventions following abuse is dominated by studies of specialist programmes, such as those using behaviour modification techniques to bring about change in parent-child interaction or programmes involving group work with parents (Cohn & Daro, 1987). This weighting in the literature towards specialist programmes can be misleading, as these interventions are not necessarily widely available, and they are certainly not the most common form of intervention experienced by abused children and their families.

The most likely form of intervention an abusing family will receive is casework and case management from a social work agency, usually the local authority social services department. Casework consists of one or more of the following components: regular monitoring of the child's welfare, practical advice and assistance to caregivers on matters such as child care and contacts with other agencies, and personal counselling to caregivers. Casework may also lead onto involvement with other services within the agency, such as nursery provision, family aides and substitute care (Gough et al., 1987; Corby, 1987). The main emphasis in this section of the literature review is upon casework services, the intervention which the current sample received most frequently.

The intervention studies discussed in this section have been chosen to illustrate the main findings in their respective area but also to highlight other important issues related to methodology, practice and policy.

Casework

One of the means used to measure the effectiveness of casework has been the rate of subsequent abuse. In a study of families who were receiving casework intervention, mainly for physical abuse or neglect, it was found that 28% of the children experienced abuse after the onset of intervention (Corby,

1987). Other studies have produced very different rates. In a major review of intervention studies by Cohn and Daro (1987) subsequent abuse was reported for between one-third and one-half of the children in the studies reviewed. A much lower rate was reported by the NSPCC: 11% of children registered in 1983 suffered abuse between the time of their registration and the end of December 1988 (Creighton and Noyes, 1989). Although the two latter studies were not concerned exclusively with casework interventions, their results do show the difficulty of using subsequent abuse rates as a measure of the effectiveness of casework intervention.

The literature suggests that approximately 20–30% of children on a representative caseload will suffer further abuse after the onset of intervention. Further work is needed not only to obtain a more reliable estimate of the subsequent abuse rate but also to determine whether particular children or families are at risk, the severity of the incidents, the nature of the abuse and whether special intervention measures should be adopted to give particular children greater protection.

At the same time subsequent incidents of abuse need to be kept in perspective. It may be wholly unrealistic to expect all abusive behaviour by parents to cease immediately casework begins. Work by the NSPCC suggests that the large majority of subsequent incidents occur within a relatively short time of the incident for which the child was registered. The average time between initial and subsequent incidents was found to be 9 months. Therefore it may be that casework requires several months before it has any impact upon parents' abusive behaviour towards children. Cohn and Daro (1987) have suggested that there may be a optimum duration for treatment of between 7 and 18 months. Intervention within this period of time showed the maximum benefit in terms of the general progress of the case and the prospensity to re-abuse.

Subsequent abuse is only one measure of the effectiveness of casework intervention. It may be that these incidents are not generally of a serious nature and begin to decline in frequency relatively soon after the onset of intervention. It is important not to let this measure obscure the other objectives of casework intervention. Lawder et al. (1984) looked at the overall progress of cases and improvements in specific problem areas. 26% of cases were defined as 'problems solved', 48% were deemed to have met with partial progress, and in only 27% of cases was there thought to be little or no progress. Magura and Moses (1984) studied casework interventions with 250 families. More than one-fifth of families reported improvements in the following areas: child discipline, child supervision, living conditions, emotional care, child conduct and parental coping. Although some problems remained in all the families engaged in the intervention, 70% of parents expressed satisfaction with the service they received.

Despite contrasting research designs it is possible to make the tentative suggestion that casework is of benefit to significant proportions of abusing families. The research questions still to be answered concern which components of casework are most effective and which families does casework most benefit. Research by Martin (1979) and Lawder et al. (1984) indicates that parents who are positively disposed toward social work intervention will have a better outcome than those parents who are ambivalent or hostile towards intervention. Rogowski and McGrath (1986) set up a discussion group for abusing parents, to which they invited staff from welfare rights, housing and social service departments. Parents reported increased confidence in their subsequent dealings with these agencies; an increased awareness of their rights and of the workings of these agencies, and an improvement in their ability to cope with stress. Although this last intervention is more structured and intensive than that which normally takes place between caregivers, social workers and other agencies, this work does show that different elements of casework intervention may have distinctive benefits. Gough et al. (1987) note that there are few data either on the nature or the effect of casework interventions. Future work in this area must not, however, analyse casework as if it were a single entity but must look at the separate effect of the different elements of this intervention. Social workers work directly with families but also liaise with outside agencies on behalf of the family. They provide specific services such as nursery places, material goods and family aides. Social workers also initiate legal interventions and substitute care. Therefore casework needs to be evaluated both as a package of services and in terms of its constituent parts.

Pre-school provision

Work by Egeland and Sroufe (1981) has shown that the effects of maltreatment can be observed in children as young as 12 months, in terms of quality of mother-child attachment. At 18 months the same sample of children were found to be more anxiously attached to their mothers and expressed more anger, frustration, non-compliance and aggression. These findings support the work of George and Main (1979) who found that abused children, as young as toddlers, assaulted both their peers and their caretakers, verbally and non-verbally, and were more likely to respond to friendly gestures with hostility.

These findings show that quite young children from abusive environments may have very definite service needs particularly in terms of their behavioural, social and emotional adjustment. Pre-school provision has been one of the means by which social workers have attempted to meet these needs. Parish et al. (1985) studied a group of children between the ages of two and a half and five years who were referred to a pre-school class designed to enhance social skills, language and motor skills. 70% of the children showed significant improvement in terms of these skills. Stephenson (1977) reported significantly greater improvements in the cognitive ability of abused children attending a special pre-school programme in Vancouver, compared to a control meeting.

In both of these studies there was a high attrition rate. In the Stephenson study 25% of families who were approached refused to cooperate in the evaluation. 28% of the families dropped out of the programme evaluated by Parish et al. before the end of treatment. Given the positive association between parental motivation and outcome (Martin, 1979), it is possible that the findings are overly positive. However, it does appear that pre-schoool provision can have a number of significant benefits in terms of children's developmental competencies. This aspect of casework may also have benefits in terms of reducing stress between parent and child and also in enabling parents to take paid employment and thereby alleviate material stress.

Future evaluations need to concentrate upon which aspects of playgroups or nurseries are important to which outcomes. Pre-school provision offers children a supportive relationship with a caring adult; an opportunity to learn basic skills in writing and in speech; social interaction with peers and stimulation through play. Different establishments may also work on different models and this may have important implications for service effectiveness. Social service nurseries, for example, are staffed by qualified nursery nurses, whereas education authority nurseries are managed by qualified teachers. Where one establishment may have an emphasis upon play the other may be more oriented to learning. Similarly, abused children may present with a number of different needs. Allen and Oliver (1982) highlighted the existence of language deficits in abused children:

> abused children lack the trust in their environment which these authors consider necessary for adequate language development; the abused child in other words is afraid to risk talking and thereby suffers language delay due to restricted practice.

Giblin (1979) compared abused children from homes with and without play materials. The former group were noted as having 'greater interest and alertness, were more positive towards on-going activities, and were less negative towards self'.

In addition to investigating the role of different elements of pre-school provision, it is important to have more data on the actual availability and take-up of this provision amongst abusing families. If, as the research suggests, pre-school provision has a powerful ameliorative influence upon abused children's developmental competencies, but has a low rate of availability or take-up, then there is obviously a need for greater development of services in this area.

Substitute placements

The placement of children in substitute care is one of the most frequently investigated forms of intervention. It is the most likely intervention to be controlled for in follow-up studies of abused children and it has been subject to a good deal of investigation in the wider child care literature. One of the earliest follow-up studies of abused children found that substitute care improved children's growth:

> In sum the data . . . strongly suggest that the normal growth potential of most of these children could be realised only when their environment was decidedly improved for a prolonged period of time (Elmer, 1967).

Gregory and Beveridge (1984) studied a group of 13 physically abused children. At follow-up children were assigned to a 'problematic group' according to whether they met any of the following criteria: attendance at a special school; had not learned to read or write, or had a score on the Bristol Social Adjustment Guide (Stott, 1974) of 16 or more. Being in care strongly predicted not being in the problematic group. The methodological problems of follow-up studies of abused children have been discussed at length in the first section of this review, where it was pointed out that there are uncertainties as to the reliability of their findings. Gregory and Beveridge (1984), for example, acknowledge that they were unable properly to control for the effect of sex in their analysis. Despite the methodological shortcomings of much of this work, there have been a number of calls in support of substitute care for abused children. Oates et al. (1984) and Calam and Franchi (1987) have argued that the return of abused children to their original homes has been either premature or mistaken.

Studies which have focused upon interventions rather than particular samples of children have produced less positive findings. Thoburn and Rowe (1988) recorded a 28% disruption rate for placements of school age children within 18 months and 5 years of placement. Stone and Stone (1983) found that nearly 50% of placements broke down in the first four weeks because of the children's behavioural problems.

It is difficult to compare the results of these studies because the research designs are so different and would almost inevitably produce contrasting results. Intervention studies also need to examine individual elements of substitute care to find out which are beneficial and which are harmful. Substitute care should offer children a stable and non-threatening home environment; a nurturing relationship with a caring adult; it should also meet a child's material and developmental needs. By measuring the quality of these separate elements and by controlling for their individual effects, it should be possible to say more about why some care placements work for abused children while others do not. Substitute care should not be taken as a unitary phenomenon. The degree of preparation a child receives eg life story books, whether a child is placed with his/her siblings or whether some siblings remain at home, may be important factors in whether a placement is successful or not.

The need to look at individual elements of placements and at placement careers was shown in the work of Lynch and Roberts (1982). This was one of the most thorough follow-up studies of physically abused children and it is of particular importance as its findings for substitute care were more critical than many of other studies reported in the literature. Their findings for residential care were particularly negative:

> There was an aura of hopelessness and helplessness surrounding these children and a feeling that their progression into delinquency was inevitable.

Children who remained at home had the best outcomes; those children who were placed in care following a hospital-based residential treatment programme had an intermediate outcome, and children who were returned home after a period in care had the worst outcome.

The literature on substitute care for abused children has produced conflicting results. It is clear that for some children being in care is very appropriate while for other children care is disastrous. However, little is known as to why care works for some children and not others. Further research is required into abused children's baseline needs and the extent to which intervention meets these needs. As Lynch and Roberts (1982) argue:

> The message is clear: to protect children's development, each child needs a well-defined, long-term treatment plan.

Casework may also involve referral to psychological and psychiatric services although literature suggests that such referrals are made relatively infrequently (Gough et al. 1988). Where these services are provided the results may be impressive. Cohn and Daro (1987), in a large scale review, found that between 50–70% of abused children showed improvements in terms of psychological, emotional and social development after having received this form of intervention. Green (1978) reviewed the impact of psychiatric treatment on a group of 20 abused children. 15 of the children, all of whom had received treatment for at least 9 months, showed improvements in terms of cognitive functioning, academic achievement and impulse control. As the children referred to these services are likely to be some of the most disturbed abused children, these findings may not be applicable to all abused children. Also it may not be appropriate, or necessary, for all abused children to receive these intensive services. What research needs to establish are the short and long term needs of abused children. Lamphear (1986) argues that more direct treatment of abused children is needed. This claim is made without the support of sound empirical evidence. As Lamphear notes, the work of Aber and Cichetti (1984) supports the principle of age-related treatment. Lamphear lists a number of other factors which may moderate the impact of abuse: its frequency and severity; the victim's perception of the abuse and the abuser; the quality of family functioning and parent-child functioning. The author goes on to make the following recommendation:

> Different treatment strategies would seem to be indicated depending on the particular combinations among these variables (Lamphear, 1986).

Given the need for reliable data on the longer term effects of abuse it seems premature to make recommendations as to the direction which interventions should take. It may be that abused children's needs are not being met. Conversely it may be shown, particularly in cases of physical abuse, that much of the 'problem' lies in the domain of the caregiver's personality and the family's domestic circumstances. Again research is needed to quantify the nature and extent of problems presented by abusing parents and families.

Behavioural programmes

Probably the largest single group of intervention studies are concerned with behaviour modification programmes. This feature of the literature is a reflection, in part, of the need to prevent further abuse and the predominance of the psychosocial model of child abuse:

> A social – psychological definition of child abuse emphasises the nature of the socialisation process that permits the use of violence as a means of interpersonal control and problem-solving (Wolfe, 1987).

A behavioural programme evaluated by Wolfe et al. (1981) consisted of parent-education programmes, therapy for individual families and group-work. The objective of the intervention was to enhance parents' ability to cope with child care demands. Parents showed significant improvements in terms of the use they made of positive reinforcement of their children's behaviour, and in the use of commands and appropriate punishment. Subsequent abuse occurred in only 2 of the 16 families which took part in the programme. In common with many behavioural programmes, the study by Wolfe et al. used a very small sample and this is a significant limitation to the value of these intervention studies. However, many of these studies have used control groups and this is not a common feature of other types of intervention study. In the Wolfe et al. study there was a significantly greater reduction in the aversive behaviour of the experimental group compared to the control group.

Reid et al. (1981) used a social-interaction model for the basis of their work with abusive parents. The aims of the intervention were as follows: to reduce the aversive behaviour of both parents and children; to reduce the frequency of child conduct disorders, and to reduce the risk of subsequent incidents of abuse. The authors noted a significant reduction in the aversive behaviours of both mothers and their children compared to a control group.

As with other intervention studies behavioural programmes are not without their methodological problems. Reid et al. (1981) warned that some of the control group may have contained undetected cases of child abuse, so the observed differences between the groups may have been an unreliable measure of the effect of the intervention. The families in the Wolfe et al. (1981) study were ordered by the court, or were likely to receive an order, to participate in a treatment programme. Therefore the findings of the study may not be applicable to all abusing families, especially those taking part in voluntary programmes. In a behavioural programme evaluated by Nicol et al. (1988), 45% of the sample of 38 families dropped out of the programme. In general though, behaviour modification programmes have been some of the most rigorous in terms of their methodology. They tend to have better baseline measures; treatment is specified more clearly and control groups are used more frequently.

Following their major review of interventions in child protection, Gough et al. (1988) concluded:

> The need for future research is not to prove the efficacy of the behavioural model, but to determine the best method for its application and its potential scope. Research . . . would inform service choices as to whether behavioural interventions would be best placed in special treatment centres or should be applied more generally within the more normal services as suggested for preventative services.

Conclusion

The literature shows that interventions after abuse may be effective in a number of ways: in reducing the rate of subsequent abuse and aversive parent and child behaviour; in enhancing children's developmental competencies, and in promoting parents' coping abilities. While the potential efficacy of intervention is clear, many issues remain to be resolved.

Although a considerable amount of research has been conducted into the effects of intervention with abusing families, little work has been carried out into the overall pattern of service provision to abused children and their caregivers. Data are available on the number of children on child protection registers and the number of children in care (Department of Health 1991a,

1991b). Every social service department in the country is required to provide a service to abused children. Surveys exist as to how long children are on child protection registers (Creighton and Noyes, 1989) and there is research on the length of time cases stay open (Corby 1987). However these measures tend to be broad summaries of casework interventions and they say little about the day-to-day work which is being done with abusing families. Further research is needed along the lines of the National Children's Home survey (1990) into service provision for abused children and young abusers. In addition to these general surveys more detailed studies of casework are needed, in order to answer questions concerning the amount of contact social workers have with families; how much of their work is spent with outside agencies; how much therapeutic work do they undertake; how frequently are nursery places provided, and how long do family aides work with families. Intervention studies inform us as to what services should be provided and what particular components of a service should be enhanced. However, without basic data on the routine work of social work agencies who are working with abusing families, it is very difficult to make recommendations as to how services should be developed.

Following on from the above point there may be a need to rationalise interventions. Different professions and areas of the country should be developing their services on the basis of findings from intervention studies rather than on an ad hoc basis.

In the first section of this review it was argued that there is still a great deal to be learned concerning the medium and long term effects of abuse. Much of the existing literature holds that abuse has a number of significant negative sequelae for children's developmental competencies. Yet as Faber and Egeland (1987) note:

> Few investigators have attempted to account for the large spread of scores, nor have they specifically examined the abused children who are functioning at the average or above level of intelligence . . . None of the outcome investigators have attempted to determine the factors that make abused children more or less vulnerable to the effects of maltreatment.

It may be that with the formal assessment set out in the Children Act 1989, there may be a better match between children's needs and service provision. There is also little information of the service needs of abusing and non-abusing parents, around which services could be developed and gaps in service provision identified. As Faber and Egeland note, parental history may have a major influence upon children's reaction to abuse:

> It is noteworthy that 29% of the abusive mothers of incompetent children were themselves abused by their husbands or boyfriends, compared to none of the mothers of the competent children.

If parental circumstances and needs have such a powerful effect upon children's reaction to abuse then this raises major questions as to who should be the recipient of services.

Although there is no comprehensive and detailed survey data on the provision of all services to abused children and their families, it is clear that the large majority of interventions are provided by local authority social service departments. A number of authors have called for more responsibility for this work to be given to other agencies (Wodarski et al. 1990). There may already be a pattern emerging of more diverse service delivery (Cox et al., 1992). Intervention studies need to establish the treatment needs of abused children and their caregivers in both the short and the long-term. Further data is needed on the overall provision of services and on the individual components of intervention which are of greatest efficacy. Taken together this research should allow for a far more rational and coherent development of services for abused children and their families.

III: LIFE EVENTS AND THE CAREERS OF ABUSED CHILDREN

Introduction

Little is known about the incidence of specific life events and the general careers of abused children. This is despite the fact that these aspects of abused children's lives may have major implications for the treatment and management of child abuse. Three areas of particular concern can be identified:

1. Subsequent incidents of abuse once a child has been officially identified as abused or at risk.

2. The effect of life events upon outcome.

3. An understanding of the broader aspects of an abused child's life.

Subsequent incidents of abuse

The first concern of child protection agencies must be the prevention of further abuse to a child. Subsequent incidents of abuse can, therefore, be seen as one measure of the effectiveness of the child protection system. Some of the earliest follow-up studies of physically abused children found alarming rates of subsequent physical abuse. Skinner and Castle (1969) reported subsequent abuse among 60% of children. Morse et al. (1970) found that 73% of children had experienced subsequent incidents of abuse. It is significant that more recent studies have recorded considerably lower rates: Hyman and Parr (1978) in a retrospective survey found that 39% of families subject to a case conference for child abuse had injured one or more of their children on a previous occasion. Re-abuse rates of between 30% to 47% were reported in US multiple site programe evaluations (Runyan & Gould, 1985). In one of the most substantial follow-ups of children registered for abuse in Britain (Creighton and Noyes, 1989) it was found that 6% of children had been subsequently abused. Much of the difference in these prevalence figures may be explained by the concentration of the more severe cases in earlier studies.

During the 1970s and 1980s children identified as abused were drawn from a much broader cross-section, and are almost certainly a more accurate representation of all abused children than were earlier samples. Consequently the lower subsequent abuse rates may be a more accurate reflection of the risk which children who remain in their original homes will face.

While the risk of subsequent abuse may not be as high as predicted by Skinner and Castle (1969) and Morse et al. (1970), it must be recognised that studies such as those carried out by the NSPCC (Creighton and Noyes, 1989) probably provide a minimum estimate. The cases studied by Creighton and Noyes were registered between 1983 and 1987 and were subject to review in December 1988. This meant that children had varying levels of exposure to the risk of subsequent abuse. The rate of subsequent abuse among the earliest children to be registered ie in 1983, was 11%. Given that the mean age of (physically) abused children in the study was 7 years, this means that each child had a further 9 years in which to be abused. It must also be remembered that the methodological problems inherent in child protection research often lead to a loss of data. Therefore the prevalence rate of subsequent abuse amongst current samples of registered children may be considerably higher than 11%.

Follow-up studies of other samples of abused children being analysed in particular child care contexts support this view. In a study of children placed home-on-trial Farmer and Parker (1991) found that approximately one-quarter of the sample experienced subsequent abuse. Again it may be argued that these latter studies focused upon groups of children and families who were particularly at risk. This raises a general issue as to whether it is possible to identify caregivers who are at higher risk of subsequently abusing their child. Indeed there are a number of questions concerning subsequent abuse which need to be addressed: such as whether subsequent incidents are perpetrated by the person responsible for the original abuse; whether the prevalence rate is inflated by excessive professional concern, and whether intervention has any effect upon the rate of subsequent abuse. The NSPCC study found the mean interval between a child's registration and subsequent abuse was nine months, with a range between one month and four years, which may indicate that intervention should be concentrated in the period around, and relatively shortly after, registration. The work by Creighton and Noyes also showed that physically abused children may go on to suffer not only further physical assault but also sexual abuse, emotional abuse and neglect, which indicates that some registered children and families may need services which are not exclusively concerned with physical violence. A great deal more needs to be learnt about the prevalence and nature of subsequent incidents of abuse.

Subsequent incidents of abuse may also occur to siblings. Creighton and Noyes (1989) found that 9% of siblings had been physically abused and 8% sexually abused. Lynch and Roberts (1982) conducted a questionnaire survey amongst social workers and GPs which revealed that of the 39 children involved in the follow-up, 8 (21%) had suffered a subsequent incident of physical abuse. However only 1 (2%) of the 41 siblings had been abused after the point when the child was officially identified as abused. These figures suggest that siblings in some families may be at differential risk of both abuse and subsequent abuse. Gil (1970) has suggested that children who are abused by their parents may possess characteristics which may make them more prone to being abused.

Similarly, parents may scapegoat one child and treat the remaining siblings with favour. Given the differences in rates of abuse by age and sex some differentiation within a sibling group is to be expected. However, given the size of the differences between siblings it is likely that other factors are involved. Studies of subsequent incidents of abuse would enable statements concerning differential risk to abuse, within sibling groups, to be made with more confidence, and would provide a platform for altering practice within families where it is felt the children are being singled out for maltreatment. One would imagine that the prognosis for such children is significantly worse and that more drastic intervention is required.

The relationship between life events and outcome

Abused children and their families have been shown to experience a much higher incidence of life events, such as separation between caregivers, moving home and separations between siblings, than the general population (Creighton and Noyes, 1989). These changes are often assumed to have negative consequences for the child's development, particularly if they occur with some regularity. Empirical evidence, however, raises a number of questions concerning the strength, direction and the causal mechanisms of the observed relationship between life events and outcome. Much of the work concerning the effects of life events has been carried out in the field of child psychiatry and developmental psychology. While abused children may be the only one of the groups studied within these frameworks, this work is still of considerable relevance.

Retrospective studies have shown a relationship between major life events and a number of different child psychiatric problems, such as conduct disorders (Vaux and Ruggiero, 1983), difficulties at school (Sandler and

Block, 1979) and depression (Swearingen and Cohen, 1985). Although relationships between events and children's adjustment can be shown, their precise meaning is open to question. In the same work Swearingen and Cohen (1989) argued that the observed relationship between events and subsequent psychiatric disorder in children is not causal but that both factors are associated with the pre-events level of psychological functioning ie stress precedes life events and is the key factor in the later observed problems of adjustment.

Other works in this field have proffered the belief that events have an effect in themselves but have suggested alternative causal processes. Holmes and Rahe (1967) saw events as having a mechanical additive effect. Brown and Harris (1978) have not altogether discounted this view but have argued that events may not have a simple cumulative effect, in that once an event of a sufficient intensity has been experienced subsequent events will prove to be of less importance to the child's adjustment. This theory is of special relevance to child abuse where some of the victims may have been severely traumatised.

Thomas and Chess (1984) have said that the relationship between events and psychological functioning is different for adults and children. In adults life events lead to distress which in turn cause psychiatric disorder. By contrast, children's reactions to life events will be heavily dependent upon their parents' response. McFarlane has raised the possibility that life events and children's psychiatric problems may both be the product of the parents' psychological disorder and lack of coping skills. Alternatively, existing psychiatric disorder in children may result in stressful life events.

Any discussion of the relationship between life events and a child's psychological adjustment is confounded by the paucity of evidence and by differences between studies in terms of the assessment techniques, measures and the time frames used (McFarlane, 1988). This leads Berden et al. (1990) to conclude:

> What does emerge from a review of the psychiatric literature is that it is essential to take into account the separate effects of life events, when considering the impact of abuse and intervention upon children's outcome.

As Rutter (1981) concludes:

> stressful events in childhood, as in adult life may cause at least short-term disturbance.

It must also be emphasised that abused children experienced a much higher number and greater range of life events (Elmer, 1967; Lynch and Roberts, 1982). Given this greater exposure to life events it may be that this group is at particular risk of adjustment problems after the life events. The literature has included abuse or persistent body injury as life events (Adams and Adams, 1991; Berden et al., 1990), but generally speaking the effect of life events with abused samples has seldom been considered. Frequent changes of address or school could, for example, have profound effects upon peer relationships or school performance. Many abused children lead lives which are best described as chaotic. The role of life events may not yet be clearly understood but it should be examined in any investigation of the impact of abuse and intervention upon a child's developmental competencies.

Chapter 9

The methodology of the study

Design of the study

The research was concerned with three periods in the children's lives:

Baseline   Circumstances of abuse and registration in 1981. Data obtained from contemporary records.

Intervention Life events and help from social agencies. Data obtained from agency records of standard 5 year period following registration.

Outcome   The situation of the children 9–10 years after registration. Data obtained by interview, questionnaire and testing.

This chapter describes the methods used for each stage of the research.

Sample

The sample consisted of all the children who were under the age of 5 years when their names were placed on child protection registers (CPR) in 1981 in one of two areas: a city, and a shire county. Drawing the sample from two areas meant it was more diverse and hopefully more representative.

(i) Size

In determining the size of the sample due regard had to be given to two conflicting requirements: the sample had to be sufficiently large such that it would be possible to conduct within-group comparisons. At the same time there was a wish to gather a large number of measures on any one individual. There were 75 children on the city CPR in 1981 and 95 on the shire county's, giving a total sample size of 170.

(ii) Age

By restricting the age range of the children being studied it was possible to arrive at a sample who were, developmentally, more homogeneous. This meant that there was a greater likelihood of finding research instruments which could be used across the whole group and that within-group comparisons would be more valid. Also by choosing a sample who were very young (under 5) at the baseline point, the amount of information on the children's lives which would be missing would be minimised.

Abuse within this age group ie 0–4 years is of particular concern given that such children are at a crucial stage in terms of the development of emotional bonds. This sample included children who had experienced severe adversity at a highly vulnerable period of their lives.

(iii) Drawing a sample from NSPCC registers

Obtaining the sample from child protection registers was just one of the means by which a sample could have been identified. It might, for example, have been possible to obtain a sample from hospital or clinic lists. However, a major drawback of such alternative sources is that they tend to focus upon particular groups, such as the more seriously injured children or higher-risk families. Children on registers exhibit a far greater range of injuries and family situations. While register samples cannot avoid all bias, they are probably far more representative of all abused children than alternative samples would be.

In addition, children on registers have been identified as being at risk and they and their families are targeted for intervention by agencies. By studying this type of sample it is possible, therefore, to evaluate the effect of this professional intervention.

As NSPCC registers were operated on a national standard it was possible to obtain a number of samples from different parts of the country which had been defined by roughly the same criteria. The definition of physical abuse used in the two study areas was:

> All physically injured children under the age of 17 years where the nature of the injury is not consistent with the account of how it occurred or where there is definite knowledge, or a reasonable suspicion, that the injury was inflicted (or knowingly not prevented) by any person having custody, charge, or care of the child. This includes children to whom it is suspected poisonous substances have been administered. Diagnosis of child abuse will normally require both medical examination of the child and social assessment.

A further advantage of using a sample drawn from NSPCC registers was the availability of information, in records, relating to the abuse and a family's circumstances at the time of the abuse.

Comparison group

A Comparison group was used in the interview stage of the study. For each index child three Comparison children, of the same age, sex, school and area of residence were identified. The majority of Comparison children were identified through the index system of the school medical service. Other Comparison children were identified by approaches to schools.

The names of all the Comparison children were checked against local child protection registers. If a Comparison child had been registered at any time or if it was known that s/he had been subject to any legal order, then s/he would be excluded from the list of names.

Once the Index family interview had been completed an introductory letter was sent to the corresponding Comparison family. The letter was sent to the parents of whichever Comparison child was closest in age to the Index child. If the parents or child refused to participate in the study, then a second introductory letter was sent out to the family of whichever Comparison child was next closest in age, and so on.

This procedure produced a group of Comparison children who were similar to the Index children on certain key characteristics, but who were not known to have been registered for abuse or to have been involved in the 'care' process. The purpose of the Comparison group was different to that of a control group in that there was no experimental manipulation. The Comparison group was used to calibrate the instruments used during the interview stage. This made it possible to compare the results for the abused children with those of a similar group of children who were not known to have been abused. Therefore, while it is not possible to be definite concerning causal links between group differences and abuse, by using such a comparison group it is possible to identify differences and to suggest that abuse (and intervention) may be explanatory factors.

It might have been possible to make the groups more similar. School and area of residence were used as a measure of social class, where it might have been more precise to use parental occupation. Similarly ethnicity could have been incorporated as a comparison factor. However, the decision taken was that the two groups should not be matched on too many variables for fear of missing real differences between children officially identified as abused and other children.

The Comparison group could have been selected by other means eg GP lists, school rolls, neighbourhood recruitment. Each of these methods involved formidable practical and scientific problems. However, the index system of the school medical records meant that Comparison children could be identified with relative ease and according to many of the key variables in which the research was interested. This was particularly so for children still living in either of the two study areas. For the remaining children approaches had to be made to the relevant health authority. Before the health authority would release information the request would have to be put before the ethical committee. This made the process extremely time-consuming, which was why, in these cases, direct approaches were made to schools for the identification of Comparison children.

Baseline data

A major advantage in using NSPCC register samples in the two study areas was the existence of comprehensive information, in register files, concerning the abuse incident and the child's family circumstances at the time.

A special data extraction form was devised by the research team to extract information from the register files in a systematic manner. In both the study areas the information in 1981 had been recorded at the time for research purposes as well as in case conference minutes. This meant the data had been recorded in a systematic manner, using uniform codes, and that they could be used with reasonable confidence in building up a picture of the children's circumstances at baseline and of the nature of the abuse.

Data on professional intervention

The period of time covered was heavily influenced by agency rules governing the destruction of records. The NSPCC normally destroys certain documents in its register files after only two years post-registration, with the entire file open to destruction after seven years. Many SSDs destroy files after seven years but some departments destroy their records before this. Although medical and health records are generally kept for longer periods, the possible non-availability of many social work records set an upper-time limit.

Social work records

Social Service Departments (SSDs) provide by far the biggest input into the child protection system. Data contained in SSD files is then of crucial importance to any study of intervention and outcomes. However keyworkers – those persons given special responsibility for a case – were not always drawn from the SSD. They also came from the NSPCC, other voluntary bodies, hospital social work departments and the education welfare service.

Exhaustive enquiries and searches were undertaken for all of these agencies in the two study areas where it was felt that agency might have information on a child and his/her family. If the child moved out of either of the study areas, letters were sent to the Director of Social Services in their new areas, to find out whether any social work intervention had taken place.

Negotiating access and the task of locating records proved to be very time-consuming. Fortunately the vast majority of register, SSD and other social work files, plus medical records, were still in existence and could be located. The quality of the information in records was generally quite high and enabled important questions on the type and degree of intervention to be addressed.

Data extraction forms were developed for use with social work records. This meant that information could be extracted from the files in a systematic and meaningful manner.

In deciding upon what information to extract from files we were influenced by a desire to obtain as much data as resources would allow. However, the data had to have some meaning in terms of either intervention and outcome, it had to have the possibility of being available in most if not all social work files, and it had to be amenable to being recorded in a systematic manner. The data extraction form was divided into 12 sections as follows:

1. Contact with family
2. Contact with other agencies
3. Referral history
4. Allocation history
5. Structure of social work file
6. Social work methods
7. Social work services
8. Referrals to specialist agencies
9a. Social work involvement prior to birth of Index child
9b. Social work involvement prior to registration of Index child
10. Summary of social work contact
11. File content

Social work files do not provide only a record of professional action. The files are also valuable sources of information on family life at registration and during the course of intervention. It is possible to learn of further instances of abuse, of other adversities the child has experienced eg physical and emotional neglect, and also to get some idea of the overriding problems and issues in a family's life eg parents' own abusive childhood, addiction, financial problems, mental problems. This information is crucial to a fuller understanding of why interventions are made, the impact of those interventions and the consequences of home life for the child's development.

Medical records

Children's medical and health records were searched, to provide further information on injury history, professional intervention and general health.

There were two main sources of medical information: hospital records, consisting of Accident and Emergency (A & E) notes and main hospital notes, where the patient had received treatment on either an in- or an out-patient basis. The main hospital notes were generally straightforward to locate. The A and E notes were more problematic as they were stored chronologically (not under the patient's name as with main hospital notes) and were liable for destruction after five years. A difficulty in tracing any medical record was knowing which hospital a child had attended. Some of the children visited hospitals in each of the three health authorities which covered each study area, and they may have visited hospitals outside the study area.

At the time of the research, community health records were made up of the individual records of community midwives, health visitors, baby clinic doctors and school nurses and doctors. The data extraction forms were designed to extract a maximum amount of information but only if that type of information could be reasonably expected to be found in most, if not all, records. This provided a comprehensive but concise and systematic record of intervention and the child's health. The format of the two instruments was as follows:

Data Extraction Forms

Medical

1. Date of visit
2. No. nights admitted
3. History at presentation
4. Diagnosis
5. Treatment given
6. Follow-up action
7. Notes

Health

1. Contact with child
2. Contact with other agency
3. Tests
4. Vaccinations
5. Injuries
6. Other health problems
7. Social information
8. Other health contacts
9. File contents

School Records

At the outset of the project it had been hoped to conduct a direct search of the children's school records. This proved not to be viable for two reasons: first the education authority in one of the areas said access would not be given without parental consent and also that the authority would have to take responsibility for seeking that consent. This was not feasible.

A second problem with school records was that the academic information they contained was not standardised between schools, let alone between education authorities. This fact on its own meant that it would not be worthwhile searching school records. Some information, concerning a child's schooling history, was obtained from schools during the interview stage of the project. This is discussed later.

Outcome measures

The interview stage represented a 9 to 10 year follow-up. Sufficient time had elapsed for distinctions to be made in terms of services received by different families, and also to show whether the abuse, and the subsequent intervention, had any effect beyond a few years.

Outcome measures were sought from five sources:

1. An interview with the child's main care giver
2. An interview with the child
3. An assessment of the child's cognitive ability and educational achievement
4. Measurement of the child's physical development
5. Completion of a questionnaire by the child's teacher

Care giver interview

In order to evaluate lasting effects on children of events in the past, it was necessary also to allow for effects on them resulting from their present-day family circumstances. The care giver interview, therefore, was intended to give a detailed picture of current influences in the child's life. For this reason it was important that the project made some attempt to assess the personal situation of at least the main care giver and also evaluate the nature of the child's home environment. However, this interview also provided information on the care giver-child relationship, from the former's perspective. Given that the study was in essence a study of the results, at least, of a dysfunctional care giver-child relationship, it was vital to investigate this area.

It was with these factors in mind, that the parent interview schedule was designed. The schedule consists of the following sections and standardised questionnaires (for references see chapter 1):

Section 1   Social information (household composition, parental occupation(s), accommodation, area)

Section 2   Social support

Section 3   Child behavioural and emotional problems, health, social life, supervision, punishment

Section 4   Care giver-partner relationship (domestic tasks distribution, decision-making, disputes)

Section 5   Family Problem Questionnaire (social, emotional and material problems)

Section 6   Malaise Inventory (Respondent's level of distress)

Section 7   Contact with services (frequency, reason, satisfaction level)

The care giver interview lasted approximately one and a quarter hours on average and interviewers asked to see the care giver alone.

Child interview

The child interview was constructed for this study with assistance from members of the Advisory Committee, drawing in particular on previous work by Dr D Quinton. It covered the following areas:

Section 1 Leisure

Section 2 Social support

Section 3 Peer relationships

Section 4 Sibling relationships

Section 5 Relationship with parents, rules, punishment

Section 6 Depression instrument

Section 7 Fears instrument

The child interview lasted on average forty-five minutes. The large majority of children had no difficulty in answering the questions and appeared to quite enjoy the experience.

Child assessment

The vast majority of assessments were carried out at school. The school base was preferred as the atmosphere was generally far more conducive to testing than were the children's homes. This arrangement also enabled the assessor to see the pair of children on a single visit. Schools proved to be most cooperative in terms of making the children and a suitable room available for the assessment. This stage of the project was always referred to as 'assessment' as it was felt that that term would be more acceptable to both children and teachers. Teachers were not aware of the nature of the study and were 'blind' the status of Index and Comparison children. The assessment consisted of the following instruments:

1. Raven's Progressive Matrices (Standard and Coloured Versions)
   To measure abstract reasoning capacity

2. The British Picture Vocabulary Scale
   To measure receptive vocabulary

3. The British Ability Scales
   The scales used were:

   Similarities   To measure reasoning ability
   Basic Number Skills
   Word Reading
   Word Definition

Children were assessed on their own. The assessments took around about one hour to complete. Children appeared to find the hour rather demanding but also quite enjoyable.

The two persons employed to conduct the assessments were qualified teachers, who had received training in the administration of the assessment. Training was provided by staff in the Centre for Educational Guidance and

Special Needs, University of Manchester. Advice on the choice of tests was sought from members of staff in the Departments of Education and Psychology at Manchester University. This advice related both to the nature of measures the project should seek to obtain and the quality of different tests. The selected tests measure both ability in the cognitive domain and attainment of a more scholastic nature. A third factor behind the choice of individual tests was that at least some of them should be particularly appealing to children. Each test also had to cover the particular age range of the sample.

Physical measures

The measuring exercise included the standard measures of height, weight and head circumference but there were, in addition, a further seven measures in order to provide a fairly sophisticated assessment of a child's physical development. The measures used in this project were drawn up on the advice of Professor R.G. Burwell.

The measuring was carried out by qualified nurses who had received special training by attending a growth clinic under the supervision of Professor Burwell. The children were measured at school and the exercise usually took no more than a few minutes. The children were asked to undress down to their underwear but to wear a gown, provided by the nurse, for the purposes of the measuring exercise.

Teacher questionnaire

The teacher questionnaire included two standard instruments: the Prosocial Behaviour Questionnaire, which measured positive aspects of a child's behaviour at school; and the Rutter 'B' Scale which measures behavioural and emotional disorder in the child. A third section of the questionnaire referred to details of a child's schooling history eg number of previous schools, ever suspended or expelled, attendance.

Children spend a significant part of their lives at school and their performance at school may heavily influence future success and teachers are ideally situated to rate aspects of their pupils' adjustment. The measures chosen had to relate to aspects of a child's character that the teacher could readily report on and which, taken together, would not take up too much of a teacher's time.

Behavioural and emotional disorders, as well as being of some considerable interest in their own right, may also impinge upon a child's academic success. It was considered vital therefore to obtain measures in these areas. The Rutter 'B' Scale was chosen for this purpose, being perhaps the most widely used and accepted instrument in this sphere of investigation.

One of the reasons for choosing the Prosocial Behaviour Questionnaire (PBQ) was that it asked the informant to comment upon positive aspects of a child's behaviour. This, it was hoped, would make the whole questionnaire more acceptable to teachers who may not have been happy at making exclusively negative comments about children. The PBQ also has only a moderate negative correlation with the Rutter Scale and as such is measuring aspects of behaviour which are more than just the opposite of those in the Rutter Scale – aspects which may have important implications for a child's social and academic success at school.

Parents were asked for their consent for the questionnaire to be sent to their child's teacher. The questionnaire takes approximately ten minutes to complete, with the first section sometimes being completed by someone other than the teacher eg the school secretary.

Recruitment Procedures

The first step in obtaining these measures was the sending of an introductory letter to a given Index family. Two to three days after this letter was sent, an interviewer would visit the family. The interviewer would explain more about the purpose and the format of the study and answer any questions the family might have. The interviewer would then, hopefully, make an appointment to conduct the care giver interview.

During the care giver interview, or once it was completed, the interviewer explained the remaining elements of the study. If the parents were agreeable to the child taking part in the project, the interviewer then explained the study to the child and asked him/her to take part. Both the main care giver and the child were asked to sign a consent form. Where a child was under a care order, this consent may have been sought from the social services department.

Once a given Index family interview was completed, an introductory letter would be sent to the corresponding Comparison family. Exactly the same recruitment procedure was followed with the exception that refusing families were substituted by the subsequent choice Comparison family.

Interviewers were double-blind in that they did not know the precise nature of the study and they did not know whether they were interviewing an Index or a Comparison family.

Once a pair of interviews were completed a letter was sent to the children's school (which was the same school for both children). The letter was addressed to the head teacher and contained a general description of the study, copies of the consent forms and a request for the enclosed questionnaires to be completed by a teacher who knew both children.

Four experienced women interviewers were employed. All had received previous interview training and had extensive experience of carrying out interviews in family settings. Specific training for the project was given during the pilot period. During the data collection period the interviewers had regular meetings with BG (in city) and CB (in County), to ensure procedures were ahdered to.

Tracing and enlisting the children

The outcome stage of the study involved tracing and securing the cooperation of 170 children who had been registered in 1981. Minimising the attrition rate for the subjects was one of the greatest methodological problems to confront the study. Attrition, in follow-up or longitudinal studies, refers to the loss of subjects either through an inability to trace them or an unwillingness on the part of subjects to take part in a study. Some follow-up studies have managed to maintain very low attrition rates (McCord, 1978) but literature reviews have revealed rates to range from 5% to 60% (Cordray and Polk, 1983). Follow-up studies of abused children have been particularly vulnerable to high attrition rates. Oates et al (1984) were unable to assess one-third of their subjects at follow-up. Martin et al (1974) lost 65% of subjects.

There are two main reasons why attrition rates are crucial to follow-up studies. Firstly, follow-up studies are costly to mount, in terms of both time, money and effort. This has a great effect upon the size of the samples which are followed up. The largest sample sizes encountered during the course of the literature review for Chapter 8 were around 50 and 60 children. These are quite small samples compared to those used in the field of delinquency, which often number several hundred, and particularly so when compared to the national studies of child development. If even the largest child abuse follow-up studies experienced high attrition rates, then the size of the sample may be so small that within-group comparison is not possible.

The second main reason why attrition rates are problematic for follow-up studies is that the 'lost' subjects may not be representative of all the subjects. Martin et al (1974) found that a disproportionate number of the families who refused to take part in their follow-up were drawn from those families who had rejected social services intervention. These families may have had a poorer outcome, such that their non-inclusion would make the results of any outcome study more positive than they should be. Furthermore, if a study is investigating the role of intervention in the development of abused children then the loss of subjects such as they would obviously be critical.

The sample size used in the current study (N = 170) was probably the largest so far used in any follow-up study of physically abused children. However, if the study were to retain the benefits of such a large sample, it was essential to minimise the attrition rate.

Tracing the children

All the children were registered in 1981. The interviews and the assessments of children's development took place in 1990 and 1991. This meant that the only addresses we could guarantee having for the entire sample were 9 or 10 years old – having been obtained from the search of register files. The length of time since registration was not the only factor which was expected to make tracing difficult. These families were known to be geographically more mobile than the norm and also to reconstitute their families more frequently (Creighton and Noyes, 1989). They were likely to have many changes of surname. A further factor compounding the problem of tracing was that of children being placed in care. It was anticipated that a significant proportion of the registered children might be adopted, fostered or be living in residential care at follow-up. Not only were there practical problems in finding these – primarily due to changes of name and changes in area of residence – but there were also problems in gaining access to their records which had to be the start of the tracing process.

Despite these difficulties the tracing exercise proved to be very successful. Table 9.i shows that all but one of the children living in Britain was traced by 1991.

Table 9.i   **Tracing the registered children**

Situation at follow-up	N	%
Traced and living in Britain	165	97
Emigrated	3	2
Deceased	1	1
Not traced	1	1
Total	170	101*

* Total does not equal 100 because of rounding.

The success of the tracing exercise was, in fact, even greater than these figures suggest. The single child who was in Britain but not traced was known to be living in the London area, and if there had been sufficient time, this child would probably have been traced. The researchers had also made progress in tracing the three emigrated children: a check in a New Zealand electoral register (in the New Zealand High Commission in London) revealed that one of the families was still at the address to which they had emigrated several years earlier. In the cases of the two other families who had emigrated – one to Australia, the other to Europe – the researchers had been able to contact the children's grandparents who would have been able to contact the family.

There were a number of factors to explain this exceptionally high rate of tracing. The first of these was the degree of access the researchers had to social work, community health and hospital records. In the earlier discussion of methodology in Chapter 3 it was stated that access to records was essential if families were to be traced. The validity of this position was proven by the degree to which information contained in files contributed to the success of the tracing exercise.

Tracing was further assisted by the support provided directly by a number of groups: here thanks must be expressed to Dr David Quinton and Pam Remon of the Institute of Psychiatry, London, who submitted the names of all the children to the National Health Service Register. The Register is a list of all persons in England and Wales who are registered with a GP. This facility proved to be very helpful in locating some of the families who were very difficult to trace. Once agency files had been exhausted in terms of their tracing potential it was possible to resort to the indexing systems – in either card or computerised form – of many of the agencies in the two study areas. This included both social work departments, one educational department, several health districts and one Family Health Services Authority. The indexing systems were a record of all persons on whom the agency had a record. Although these systems contained only basic information, such as name and address, they were usually more up to date than files. Indexes were a valuable aid to tracing, particularly if a child had moved out of an area.

Tracing was, therefore, greatly assisted by the access the study was able to have to a number of formal recording systems: agency records, the National Health Service Register, and agency indexing systems. These formal systems may have accounted for tracing a very large proportion of the registered children, possibly as high as two-thirds or even three-quarters. However, if tracing rates of 80%, 90% or higher were to be achieved, it was necessary to call upon the ingenuity and tenacity of the researchers and the interviewers. Tracing may be viewed as a three-stage process: the first stage relied upon the formal avenues described above; if this stage did not locate a child, efforts moved onto a second stage which consisted of systematic searches or enquiries with a variety of sources: schools, health centres; neighbours, housing departments, telephone books and directory enquiries, and electoral registers. This second stage might have accounted for 90% or more of the children being traced. In order to locate the complete sample, as was nearly accomplished in this study, it was necessary to move onto a third stage. The third stage involved the research and interview staff in pseudo-detective work where they would sift through all the available information for any leads it might provide. At this stage very speculative enquiries would be made in case any of these might be useful, eg stopping people in the street, near to where a family used to live or reading through thousands of names in an electoral register. Although somewhat simplistic it could be said that there were 3 levels of difficulty in terms of tracing: little difficulty, moderate difficulty, and extreme difficulty – these levels corresponding to the three-stages described above. Case vignettes are provided to illustrate each of these difficulty levels:

Little difficulty:

A computerised search in the local education authority revealed Sarah's school and home address. The interviewer (CS) visited this address but did not receive a reply. A neighbour informed CS that Sarah's mother would be at home that afternoon. CS returned in the early evening of the following day and completed the interview there and then.

Moderate difficulty:

David's most recent address had been obtained through the search of social work records. David's mother had a psychiatric illness and was squatting in the property, with an eviction order against her being prepared. As a result, she was reluctant to answer the door and was very isolated from the neighbours. A total of 15 visits were made to this address, along with enquiries being made of neighbours and numerous notes being left, asking David's mother to contact the research office.

On the final visit to this address, a neighbour informed the interviewer (DK) that David and his mother had finally moved. Enquiries were made with the community health unit of the local health district and with David's former school (identified following a conversation with a neighbour). Neither agency knew of David's new address. The day after these enquiries had been made, the Head teacher at David's former school rang the research office to say that he had been contacted by the Head teacher of a primary school in the neighbouring local authority who said David had just joined the school. A telephone call was made to this Head teacher, but he was not prepared to divulge David's current address. However, he did mention that David was now being cared for by his grandparents. As the search of social work records had already provided the address of the grandparents, tracing David was now complete.

Extreme difficulty:

The search of records provided an address for Michelle which was only 1 or 2 years old. However, on visiting the address, the interviewer (HG) found that the family had moved. The current occupants had no idea as to where the family had moved; neither did the occupants of five neighbouring properties.

A telephone call was then made to Michelle's last known school – also identified through the records search. The Head teacher confirmed that Michelle had left the school and she suggested two possible new schools. The first of these proved to be the school to which Michelle had moved. Unfortunately, Michelle was at the school for only a few weeks before moving on again. The Head teacher did not know to which school she had moved, but he did have a more recent home address for Michelle.

HG then visited this subsequent address only to find it, and several neighbouring properties, in a derelict state. HG was able to contact one person who lived relatively close to Michelle's address but he knew nothing of the family.

The search of social work records had given the home address of Michelle's grandparents. HG then visited this address. The grandparents, however, had moved. Again the current occupants and several of the neighbours knew little of the persons being traced, although one did say that the grandparents had moved to Wales.

Perhaps in desperation, HG stopped a woman in the street who was walking past the grandparents' former home. This woman advised HG to try a house in a neighbouring street. The occupants of this house knew Michelle's grandparents quite well. In fact, a daughter of this family – who happened to be visiting at the time – lived in the same street as Michelle's uncle. This address was passed on to HG, who immediately visited it. Michelle's uncle was rather suspicious of HG, but he finally agreed to release his brother's (Michelle's father's) address. On her second visit HG found Michelle's father at home and he agreed to take part in the study.

As a postscript to this account, it should be noted that between the time of the interview and the school-based assessment, a matter of a few months, Michelle changed addresses twice and school once, thereby necessitating further tracing.

The success of the tracing exercise in this study has shown that, even with what was, for a follow-up for physically abused children, a large sample, it is possible to trace an extremely high proportion of subjects. This success was based upon a number of factors: the degree of access to records; the assistance of local and outside agencies; and the resources which the study was able to devote to the problem of tracing.

However, one of the most significant factors was the commitment of the interviewers and the research staff to the task. Murphy (1990) has argued that the problem of attrition is often treated in a very marginal manner in reports emanating from longitudinal studies, despite the fact that attrition may have a very deleterious effect upon the quality of data. All the workers on the current project were committed to the objective of tracing and securing the cooperation of as high as proportion of the original sample as was possible. For the interviewers this was a particularly onerous task as it involved having to approach numerous strangers, repetitive visits and sometimes work in hostile physical environments. Steeh (1981) has shown a steady increase in attrition rates in social surveys since the 1950s. Hopefully the current study will go some way to show that follow-up studies, even with groups which are known to be particularly difficult to trace, are not only feasible, but can, in terms of tracing – which is an important factor in data quality – be highly successful.

Children who had left the study area

It was assumed that families who had left their respective study area would be more difficult to trace as it would not be possible to use the full range of local tracing methods. From the theoretical perspective it was important to consider whether movement out of the study area affected outcome.

Just under one-third of the children had moved out of the study area by the time of follow-up. Although no systematic analysis has been conducted into the effort required to trace these 'movers' compared to the remaining children, the distinct impression is that they were not any more difficult to trace. There were a number of reasons for this. Firstly, virtually all of the adopted children and most of the fostered children, along with the single child in residential care, were outside their study area at follow-up. Adoptive families were relatively easy to trace as they tended to be fairly stable and if they had moved they belonged to quite a sophisticated social network in terms of neighbourhood, employment or services, so that it was not difficult to find someone who knew of their subsequent whereabouts. Children in foster homes or residential care were traced almost automatically as the SSD would have to have their address. Slightly more than one half of all movers consisted of children who had been placed in substitute homes. Some of the families who had moved were still receiving social services intervention. While this might have been thought to have made tracing more difficult, the converse was true.

However, some families were more difficult to trace as a result of having moved out of the study area. One such family had moved to a small town in a rural area outside England. Despite exhaustive enquiries with the social service departments, housing departments, health departments, numerous schools and even a travellers' camp, it had not been possible to trace the family. Further tracing efforts were largely frustrated, as the research office was in England, thereby making speculative field visits to the family's former neighbourhood unfeasible. In desperation, a member of the research staff (BG) rang the local library for the new area and asked for a list of the names of all the families who lived in properties neighbouring the family's former home (the address of which was known). A call was then made to directory enquiries for the telephone numbers of all these neighbouring families. All the persons who had phones were then telephoned by BG and asked whether they knew anything of the family's current whereabouts. Eventually contact was made with a man who believed that the family had moved to another town, but he added that the maternal grandfather still lived in this town. He said that next time he saw him he would pass on a message. A week later the child's mother contacted the research office, having received a message from her father via the former neighbour.

While moving outside the study area may not have been associated with increased difficulty of tracing, it did cause problems in terms of access to records. As previously explained, obtaining access to records in the two study areas was exceedingly demanding in terms of time and energy. Many of the children acquired additional records in the areas to which they moved. It was particularly important for the project to search any subsequent social work records. The children also had further hospital and community health records. As with GP records, community health records should follow children as they move between areas. Often this did not happen meaning that a child's record was divided between two or more areas.

While searching the records of the movers made a major demand upon the project, so did the task of actually obtaining permission to see the files. Contact was made with 10 social service department and 21 health districts outside the study area for the purposes of access to records and information on children's whereabouts.

One of the factors most strongly associated with the difficulty of tracing was a family's lifestyle. Geographical mobility was significant but more important than this was the context in which a family moved. Some of the families who proved to be the most difficult to trace were those who lived outside mainstream society, with an itinerant lifestyle. It was this factor, ie how they moved, rather than where they moved, which made tracing so difficult.

Given the level of movement out of the study areas, it is important to ask whether the move had any effect upon outcome. It was clear that the families (or children) moved for a number of reasons. As has been explained, over one-half of the children were moved out of the study area as a result of being placed in substitute care. For these children moving had many aspects. Adapting to new parents and a new family was perhaps the greatest issue in the children's lives. However, the move also involved other important but more subtle changes. There were, for example, black children who were adopted by white parents who lived in almost exclusively white areas, whereas the children had come originally from fairly ethnically mixed areas. At follow-up it was clear that some of these children were experiencing problems in integrating in a peer group that was all white. For children who remained in their original homes, moves out of the study area may have been beneficial particularly if the family was moving away from a problem area or moving to an area where they could expect greater support from family and friends. Some families did move back to more familiar areas but sometimes this meant moving into problem areas. Other families moved as a result of a care giver's new relationship and some families may have moved in an attempt to distance themselves from the events and problems which resulted in the child being registered. On an impressionistic level it appeared that while a move could have represented a major life change for the family, it was not the move itself which was important in terms of outcome, but the context in which it was made.

Enlisting families in the survey

Being able to trace virtually all the subjects meant that half of the battle against attrition had been won. Having found the families we had to obtain their agreement to take part in the study. Although the recruitment of families did not involve an effort on the scale of the tracing exercise, it did have to be carefully prepared if attrition was to be kept to a bare minimum.

The recruitment of a child and his/her main care giver began with the introductory letter. The construction of this letter might be thought of as a tedious business. However, while the study might have been able to achieve a respectable recruitment rate with no great effort, to achieve a very high response rate required a very carefully planned approach to parents. Even after the standard introductory letter was produced, decision would be taken as to whether individual caregivers would be addressed as Mr and Mrs . . ., Ms . . ., by their first surnames, etc.

Perhaps the single most important factor in the success of the recruitment process was the social skill of the interviewer. The interviewers were selected, in part, on the basis that they had considerable previous experience in research which involved recruiting subjects. The interviewers were also selected for their commitment to the principle that refusals should be kept to an absolute minimum. The success of the interviewers in this objective is indicated in Table 9.ii.

Table 9.ii   **Enlisting families in the study**

Description (children)	N	%
Interviewed	144	85
Not interviewed	21	12
Emigrated	3	2
Not traced	1	1
Deceased	1	1
Total	170	101*

* Total does not equal 100 because of rounding.

The actual degree of success in recruiting families is even greater than that suggested by the figures in Table 9.ii as not all the 'not interviewed' children were refusals. In the case of 3 of the 21 children, access was withheld by others. One child was the subject of a Wardship Order following the breakdown of his fostering placement amidst allegations of sexual abuse. Following a very drawn out and time consuming period of negotiation with the social services department and the local authority legal department, an application for access to the child concerned was finally made to the Wardship Judge, who did give permission. Unfortunately, the file containing the documents authorising access was mislaid almost immediately after the decision had been taken, and still had not turned up by the time interviewing was drawn to a close. The second child who could not be included in the study was also going through a traumatic fostering at the time of the follow-up. The social workers responsible for the girl asked that no approach be made to her as she was showing signs of serious emotional disturbance which was threatening the continuation of the fostering placement – which had existed for a number of years. Several months later a second approach was made to the social services department. Unfortunately, the situation had deteriorated, leading to the breakdown of the fostering placement and meaning that an interview was even less appropriate. The third child was suspected of having been the victim of organised child sexual abuse. As police and social service enquiries were still proceeding, the research staff were asked not to contact the family. Many months later, when these enquiries had not found any evidence of organised abuse – although the girl concerned was known to have been abused by her baby-sitter – the social services department gave their approval for contact with the family. Again, however, this approval came too late, as the interviewing stage had finished.

Given the results of both the tracing and recruitment exercise, the research finds itself in something of a paradoxical situation. At the outset of the study it was generally accepted by all those involved with the project that tracing and recruitment would be very formidable problems. Having achieved considerable successes in both these areas there might now be a temptation to radically alter estimations of the difficulty of tracing and recruitment. It might be useful therefore to reemphasise that tracing and recruiting such families, particularly over long periods is a major undertaking. The results of this study should not be taken as evidence that these tasks are straightforward, but rather that with adequate access to records, the support of a number of agencies, and skilled and committed staff, then these problems can be overcome.

The cases of the three children to whom access was not possible serve to illustrate some of the difficulties which arise. The study had to contend with a number of children whose circumstances were similarly precarious but where, fortunately, access was possible. Access was negotiated for one child who was in a therapeutic residential community; to children who were creating major difficulties for their adoptive parents, and to one child whose parent was quite traumatised by a recent incident of sexual abuse of the child by her grandfather. Interviewers used a range of skills to recruit these families but their efforts could usefully be summed up as a process of gaining the confidence and trust of parents and children.

As a result of searches of social work records a number of children were identified as particularly sensitive cases. The social service departments responsible for these children were contacted for their advice on whether, and how, the children and their caregivers should be approached. Another sensitive issue was that of access to adoption records. Without such access it would have been virtually impossible to trace adopted children and an important sub-group would have been lost to the project. Before this access was granted the researchers had to obtain authorisation from the Secretary of State for Health, and had to sign confidentiality forms from individual social service departments.

While certain children and families were considered to be in particularly sensitive situations, there was also a general air of sensitivity surrounding the project as a result of the ethical issues previously described. That it was possible to overcome the large majority of these problems was due, in part, to the interviewers' skills. The fact that all four interviewers were female also probably helped as most of the main caregivers were women and the interview schedule contained a number of personal issues. The interview schedules and assessment instruments were designed to be as non-threatening and 'user-friendly' as possible. Therefore when key workers, heads of homes or parents themselves vetted the research instruments, as was sometimes requested, there was little chance that they would find any item or topic so objectionable that they declined to take part in the study. This last point is important as it serves to illustrate that 'recruitment' does not stop at the start of the interview. No matter how well designed the instrument and the degree to which distressing topics are avoided, individuals may still find the interview, or test situation, anxiety-provoking. It is the interviewer's responsibility to maintain the trust and confidence of subjects throughout their time together in order to maximise the honesty and the accuracy of the data. The children usually consented to take part in the study as a matter of course, but the interviewers were still instructed to obtain their formal agreement. The researchers felt that children's individual consent should be obtained as a matter of principle. However, it was also hoped that it would serve a useful purpose in that it would give power to the child which in turn might enhance rapport between the interviewer and child, and ultimately lead to more reliable answers.

The characteristics of the non-participant children

It was stated above that one of the problems of attrition is that it may lead to bias in the results. This problem is not considered to be very significant in the current study as the proportion of children and caregivers who did not participate was quite small (15%).

Ultimately it is impossible to be precise as to what effect the non-inclusion of particular families may have had, for the simple reason that very little is known about their current circumstances. It is possible, though, to look at the characteristics of the non-participants to see how their removal may have altered the representativeness of the final sample.

Table 9.iii shows that in terms of age at registration there was little difference between the non-participants and the sample as a whole.

Girls were more likely to be non-participants (Table 9.iv). This trend was evident amongst both the group of 7 children who were not available for interview (3 where permission could not be obtained for access to the child; 3 emigrated children, and 1 not traced) and the group of 18 children who were actual 'refusers'. Fortunately, the numbers involved are relatively small and should not have had too great an effect upon the results (which are able to take into account sex because of the matching process). However, it may be that the difference in the numbers of refusals from the parents of boys against girls (6 and 12 respectively), suggests that parents may be more protective towards girls than boys. This could have had an effect in the interviews with parents being more reticent about providing information about their daughters, particularly where it is negative. At the time that the field work was

Table 9.iii **Comparison of complete sample and non-participants' age at registration**

Age at registration (years)	Complete sample (%)	Non-participants (%)
<1	30	31
1–2	42	38
3–4	28	31
Total	100	100

Table 9.iv **Comparison of complete sample and non-participants' sex distribution**

Sex	Complete sample (%)	Non-participants (%)
Male	56	31
Female	44	69
Total	100	100

being conducted there was nationwide concern over bogus officials attempting to gain access to children in their own homes. Anxiety over this matter was raised by a number of parents and so it may have influenced the response of parents to the study.

In the course of record searches and our attempts to recruit families it had been possible to accumulate data concerning some basic elements of the non-participant children's recent circumstances, which might be thought to be of particular relevance to their status at outcome. It must be said that this data is limited. However, a number of interesting points can be made. The first is that many of the children had encountered quite major events in their lives. Seven children had been adopted (including one of the emigrated children) and another was awaiting adoption; two further children had emigrated; one child was the subject of a wardship case and was in residential care; one child had recently experienced a fostering breakdown and another had been sexually abused by her babysitter; and one girl had experienced the death of her birth mother. In a number of the remaining cases there may not have been such dramatic events but there was some evidence that the children's lives had been fairly chaotic. So it may have been the case that some of the non-participant children had poorer outcomes. However several of the non-participant children appeared to have quite ordinary lives. Indeed an early analysis of response rates showed that the Index families were more likely to cooperate than the Comparison families. So it may have been that the Index families who refused to participate in the project share more of the characteristics of the Comparison group. It must also be said that some of the non-participant children were known to have had good outcomes. One girl, for example, who was at the time of follow-up awaiting adoption, had been sexually abused by her former social worker and three family acquaintances. Her original home life had been striking for its lack of physical and emotional care. Despite these adversities both her prospective adoptive parents and her current social worker reported the girl's emotional, behavioural and educational adjustment to be very satisfactory. In short, it is difficult to identify particular trends amongst the non-participant children. While major life events were over represented, there were many differences within this group. From the mass of information which had been obtained through record searches and tracing the children, it could not be said that there were any strong trends that might have affected the children's developmental competencies. Our impressions were that the children covered a fairly broad spectrum.

Chapter 10

Conclusions

We must now try to draw together and interpret the results. First we should consider how far methodological problems have been overcome, starting with attrition from the sample.

Methodological issues

All but five of the 170 children placed on registers in 1981 were traced to an address in 1990/91 by BG. Of the five, three were abroad, one had died a 'cot death' at a few months old and in one case the address could not be found in the time available. Tracing was remarkably successful, especially given the high mobility and frequent name changes of the children. Attrition due to refusal to participate in the study was also quite low. Only 18 families refused and three children were withheld by social services departments. Thus only 15% of the original sample were lost from the study.

This could still be serious if there were reasons to think that the missing children were particularly unusual. They included a higher proportion of girls but they were much the same in age and on the measures of risk that existed at the time of registration in 1981. However, it is possible that the three children in the care of social services who were withheld were marked by particularly horrific subsequent experiences which might have been associated with worse outcomes. If anything therefore, their loss from the study might have meant an overestimate of the success of children removed from their own families.

Baseline data from 1981 records were available on all the children, but had the drawback of having been collected by many different people who might have been using different standards and been more or less thorough. Records of the key agency were available for the whole follow-up period in nearly three-quarters of cases and were completely missing in only 7%. Again, these records had not been kept for research purposes and although they were surprisingly comprehensive in nearly all cases, their limitations must be recognised. Any bias must be in the direction of understating the amount of contact and service given.

We hoped to achieve a Comparison group equivalent in age, sex and social class distribution. By selecting a group who lived in the same neighbourhoods as well as attending the same schools this was achieved. By checking official records we were able to exclude Comparison children who had come to the notice of the child protection register — quite a few of the original selections had to be replaced for this reason. However, it may be that some of the Comparison children had suffered abuse that was never officially recognised.

On the whole, we believe that the amount of bias introduced by attrition from the sample, absence of recorded data and inappropriate Comparison children was relatively small. Bias was also reduced by ensuring that interviewers and teacher raters were blind to the status of the children, and also aware of the purpose of the study only in general terms.

Outcomes

The children's status on measures of development was evaluated nine to ten years after registration – a long follow-up period by the standards of much previous research. However, in terms of the whole of the children's lives, it is still early days: their average age was only eleven. The picture of the children's development may well change as they reach adolescence.

The follow-up period was long enough for the immediate turbulence following the official recognition of abuse to have died down. One of the encouraging things about the study was the apparent stability of nearly all the children's living circumstances at the time of the follow-up interview. Only one of those interviewed was in residential care (though one of the missing cases was also in residential care after breakdown of a previous arrangement). The vast majority (some 99%) were in stable family situations, an excellent outcome for the child protection system.

However, these children had already endured more losses and changes than most people encounter in a lifetime. Under a quarter still had the same parent figures that they had had ten years before; nearly half had changed one parent; and 29% had completely new parents. Most had lost original siblings and/or gained new ones. Many children had experienced frequent changes of address and school as a result of official intervention in their lives or of parental mobility. Again though, study of these life events suggested that most of the turbulence had occurred in the years immediately following registration. By the time of follow-up, nine to ten years later, most lives had stabilised. This may be why the amount of change experienced by children (or at least those changes mentioned in official records) had no clear influence on their scores on the measures of development at follow-up.

Measures of development

We evaluated children's outcomes by comparing their progress on various measures of development with that of the Comparison children who had never been officially recognised as abused. Our results are in line with the majority (though not all) of previous research, in finding significant differences between physically abused and Comparison cases after controlling for the effects of social class and disadvantage.

The most important differences were in **behaviour**, as rated by parents in the home and teachers in the school. The formerly abused children (boys and girls) were more likely in both settings to display behaviour problems. They were significantly more restless and fidgety; more miserable, solitary and unpopular; more prone to lying, fighting, stealing and destroying property. Formerly abused boys were also identified by teachers as having more emotional problems than Comparison boys. Teachers rated formerly abused girls as having significantly fewer prosocial or desirable forms of behaviour in the school setting. In general, teachers (but not parents) rated boys in both Comparison and Index groups as having more behaviour problems than girls.

On the scales used, the Comparison as well as the Index children showed more behaviour problems than would have been expected in the general population of children. This may have been due to the matching of Index and Comparison children on social class and inner city residence.

Index children reported significantly more **friendship problems** than Comparison children, complaining more of bullying, need for and lack of people to play and do things with, although there were no differences in absolute numbers of people classed as friends.

There were some, but not large, differences in **intelligence and educational attainment**. Index children were more concentrated in the lower percentile ranges on a standard test of abstract reasoning. Although both groups showed depressed performance in comparison with the general population on tests of reading and number, the Comparison boys performed significantly better than the Index ones on all but the Word Reading Test and Comparison girls performed somewhat better on all tests. The relatively low scores of the Comparison children compared with general population norms was probably again due to the matching procedure, since social class status had a significant influence on cognitive test scores.

Again, the results are in line with the majority of previous studies. However there was no support for the finding of Calam & Franchi (1987) that abused girls had better than normal educational performance.

There were no differences between the physical growth of Index and Comparison children, although a higher proportion of the Index group may well have been small at birth. In the longer term any physical growth lags had apparently been caught up. No other studies have demonstrated long-term delayed growth in abused children.

A statistician, who had no other knowledge of the children, used the different measures in order to develop an outcome profile for each child. Three outcome clusters were identified: 'Good' – Low parent and teacher ratings of behaviour problems, good educational performance and absence of self-reported fears and depression; 'Poor' – Many behaviour problems, low educational achievement and above average fears and depression scores; 'Low

Performance' – An intermediate group with relatively poor educational achievement but fewer behaviour problems and self-reported symptoms.

This summary measure clearly distinguished Index from Comparison children. Only 22% of the Index had a good outcome (compared with 48%); 42% had a poor outcome (19%); while the proportions in the low performance group were similar (36% v. 33%). There was a considerable overlap between the two groups, with approaching a fifth of the Comparison children having a poor outcome, and just over a fifth of the formerly abused having a good one. Physical abuse did not necessarily lead to developmental problems in the longer term.

This point is re-inforced by the finding that the best (statistical) discrimination between the Index and Comparison children correctly classified only 68% into the 'right' group – 33% better than would have been achieved by chance. A substantial minority of Comparison children, where abuse had never been identified, had serious behavioural and educational problems, while some formerly abused children had no identifiable problems nine to ten years later. We found substantial numbers of children apparently developing in distorted ways, regardless of whether or not they had been abused in early life.

Effects of the original abuse on Index Children's development

If the experience of physical injury in early life has specific long-term effects, one would expect that the circumstances in which injury occurred, its seriousness for example, would have some predictive power. We were able to test this since contemporary NSPCC records of the circumstances of the abuse and the case conference survived. Only a minority of the children (16%) suffered serious injury. Within this group, four suffered some degree of brain damage and in their cases specific long-term consequences were observable in the form of cognitive impairment and the need for special education. Otherwise seriousness of injury had no apparent effect. Indeed, about 14% had never been injured at all but were registered 'prodromally'. They had no better outcomes than the injured children.

There was some evidence that combined neglect and abuse, and widespread family violence, might have more serious long-term consequences. Other research has suggested that neglect has particularly damaging effects on children's development (Egeland et al., 1983; Wodarski et al., 1990). On the whole though, circumstances existing at the time of abuse were not useful predictors of outcomes ten years later, probably because so many changes had occurred in the children's lives in the interim.

Repetition of abuse

At a minimum estimate, 24% of the Index children had been subsequently physically or sexually abused following registration – a figure that is on the low side in comparison with other studies. Subsequent physical abuse was concentrated in the two years following registration. It very rarely caused serious injury. Any repetition of abuse usually triggered prompt protective action, to remove the perpetrator or remove the child, and this was one reason for the instability in the children's lives in the period following registration.

There was no evidence that children who suffered subsequent abuse had worse or better outcomes on the measures of development. This finding is again consistent with the view that physical abuse, in itself, is unlikely to have specific longer-term consequences.

However, there were some real differences between the behaviour and cognitive performance of the children who had suffered early abuse and those who had not, even after allowing for social status differences. We have argued that there was no evidence that early injury in itself (unless it led to brain damage) caused any specific long-term harm to children. Nevertheless, early injury recognised by community agencies as serious enough to require registration could have been a marker for ongoing child-rearing problems that had a persistently harmful effect. In addition, registration and protective actions (by parents as well as officials) often led to de-stabilising periods in children's lives and loss of significant figures. A chain of events was sometimes set in motion that could lead to severe material disadvantage for the child living with a lone mother. In other words, although the present-day circumstances of the Index children had often come about, in a step by step way, as a result of those events nine to ten years ago, present-day circumstances rather than past traumatic events appeared to have more direct influence on the children.

> a life of early adversities can have a number of diverse outcomes, with long-term effects heavily dependent on the nature of subsequent life experiences. (Rutter et al, 1990)

Present-day social circumstances and family relationships

Social disadvantage

At the time of follow-up, formerly abused children were significantly more likely to be living in conditions of poverty, and to be in households headed by lone parents, although their social class distribution was no different from that of the Comparison children.

Children in higher social classes (whether Index or Comparison) had significantly better results on the measures of educational performance, while those with greater social disadvantage had significantly worse ones on a range of measures. Lone parenthood showed no independent association with children's outcomes. The excess lone parenthood in the Index sample was partly a consequence of the abuse itself. It reflected the success of one parent in ridding (usually) herself of a violent partner, but often the price to be paid was living in poverty.

Mobility

Index children had significantly more changes of address in the last five years and had been at their present address for significantly shorter periods. Neither of these factors showed any independent association with children's outcomes. The excess mobility in the Index group was again probably a consequence of the abuse, illustrating the turbulence caused by official recognition and efforts to improve the children's welfare.

Parenting

Parenting can be seen as a task requiring a number of skills, both of a practical and of an interpersonal kind. We were particularly interested in methods of discipline and in evidence of parents' affection, concern and involvement with their children.

We attempted to identify parental styles in Index and Comparison groups through a series of questions in the interviews with the main care giver and the child. Parenting styles at the time of follow-up were strongly related to children's scores on the measures of development in both groups. When parents had predominantly critical, punitive styles and used more physical punishment children had more behaviour problems, higher depression scores and more friendship problems. On the other hand, children who saw their parents as strict and those who had warmly positive relationships with them had fewer behaviour problems and better cognitive performance. They were less likely to do well if they saw parental discipline as inconsistent and parents as unreliable and showing little warmth and affection.

Index children were more often exposed to apparently harmful punitive parenting styles and received more physical punishment. However, we cannot conclude that parenting behaviour had a directly causal effect on children's outcomes. It is possible that children and parents were sometimes trapped in 'coercive' interactions of the sort described by Patterson (1982). In such a pattern, children's difficult or antagonistic behaviour elicits hostile and aggressive responses from the parent which in turn escalate the level of the child's defiance. Other research has suggested that the abuse incident itself may not be the cause of distortions to children's subsequent development.

Day-to-day unpleasant interactions with parents and a generally coercive style of parenting may be more important (see Lamphear, 1986 for a review). The evidence from the present study points in this direction.

The main care givers of the Index children were more burdened with emotional and practical problems, felt more isolated and were less satisfied with the social support available to them. There was more violence between the adult partners in the Index families. The stress on the adults in the family may have had indirect effects on the Index children.

It seemed clear that social disadvantage, family problems and parenting styles had some association with children's behaviour, regardless of whether they had been abused. These factors may also have accounted for some of the differences between Index and Comparison children. However, the factors were inter-correlated and it was not possible to establish a statistical model that would enable causal explanation. It would not be possible to predict with confidence that the results in another sample would be the same as the ones found in this study. Thus the relationships found here could not be used to predict children's outcomes in any generalised way. Rather, they suggest specific hypotheses to be tested in future, more focused research.

Children in substitute families

Of the forty-two children in more-or-less permanent substitute care at the time of follow-up, 17% were fostered with relatives, 38% with non-relatives, 43% were adopted and one child was in residential care. The children in substitute care did not differ greatly from the remainder in characteristics present at the time of the original abuse, but their families were poorer and parental neglect had more often been recorded.

Adopted children had been in their families for at least seven years, having mostly been placed before the age of three. Foster children had joined their families at older ages on average and had been in them for less long. No clear relationships could be found between children's ages at placement and their outcomes. The whole 'separated' group had generally moved from the most disadvantaged circumstances at the time of abuse to the most privileged at the time of follow-up. The material outcome for 'separated' children was very good.

There was a consistent trend for adopted children to show more behaviour problems, more friendship problems and more depression compared with children in foster care. Adoptive parents tended to feel more depressed and isolated from support. They were more likely to be using punitive parenting styles and physical punishment and this could have had a bearing on the adopted children's relatively more disturbed behaviour.

No child was physically abused in a substitute family, but one was in a residential home.

The influence of protective services

When considering the services received by the children and their families, it must be remembered that the findings refer to the mid-1980s. Patterns of service delivery have no doubt changed to some extent since then.

Analysis of records kept by the key agency during a standard five year follow-up period revealed a general picture of long periods of allocation; a huge amount of direct face-to-face and phone contact; and a surprising degree of continuity of service. Most families received several supportive services (usually consisting of day care and/or help in money or in kind). The key social worker usually had a great many contacts with other agencies in order to monitor the children's progress. The typical picture was of a conscientious social worker going to great lengths to keep in regular contact with the child and family, monitoring and helping in practical ways as financial, marital or other crises arose.

Social workers made little use of formal social work methods. Nor did they often refer children (or parents) for direct treatment services.

For children who remained with their own parents, there was some evidence that more intensive and prolonged social work contact related to better outcomes. For adopted children, however, the opposite was the case. For children who remained with natural parents, packages of service that included psychiatric treatment for an adult, therapeutic attendance at a family centre and support from a voluntary agency, appear to have benefits. The use of legal orders did not discriminate between children with good and poor outcomes. However, the majority of the 'effective' service packages for children in their own homes had been supported by a legal Order, which pobably secured access to more resources.

Implications of the results

The study was motivated by our wish to provide information that would improve decision-making in child protection work. We hoped to find predictive indicators that would give clear pointers to the need for protective intervention. Instead we found little sign that the severity of physical abuse (except when it caused brain injuries) or its context, or the level of other adverse early experiences had any direct effects on children's development nine to ten years later. These early experiences had often set in motion a chain of events that had led step by step to the child's present situation. It was present day circumstances and relationships that seemed to have most effect on children's present day behaviour. Similarly, we found no clear-cut general rules that would make decision-making about the placement of children much easier. *Within* each form of placement – adoptive, foster care or natural parent – there was so much variation in children's outcomes that clear differences *between* the groups did not emerge. A child might do well in any of the three. Much therefore depended on careful and sensitive assessments in individual cases.

The follow-up study identified an important minority of school-aged children who were often in stressed and socially disadvantaged families; and who were personally unhappy, low achievers who displayed troublesome behaviour at home and school. These children generally received more physical punishment in their homes, were exposed to more punitive parenting styles, and were less warmly involved with their parents. Children who had been abused in early life were over-represented in the group, but it included other children as well.

These difficulties may just represent a passing phase in the children's lives, but it is quite possible that they forecast an excess chance of further social failure in adolescence and adulthood. Research evidence suggests that such children are more likely to become delinquent (Gray, 1988; Widom, 1989); they may have difficulties in forming stable relationships and may in turn become unsuccessful parents (Egeland et al, 1984).

The evidence from this study points away from the conclusion that physical abuse in early life had a directly causal influence in producing the children's developmental problems. It seemed rather that physical abuse was, in some cases, an important 'marker' for continuing adverse conditions, including perhaps most importantly a harshly punitive, less reliable and less warmly involved style of parenting. If this is right, more attention needs to be paid to these adverse conditions in assessing the need for intervention at the time when physical abuse is uncovered. A physical assault (even if serious), in the absence of serious family problems and a coercive parenting style, is less likely to have long-term consequences. At present, policy and practice perhaps emphasise too much the protection of the child from physical danger, and too little the need to find ways of intervening in order to promote children's longer-term development.

It is easy to forget how recent have been the developments that have put child protection at the centre of local authority social services departments' provision for children and families. Until the 1970s, welfare promotion and the prevention of juvenile delinquency were the policy priorities for the (then) Children's Departments (Harding, 1991). The death of Maria Colwell at the hands of her stepfather in the early 1970s introduced a 'protectionist' trend, strengthened by the recognition in the 1980s of child sexual abuse as a not uncommon occurrence. Inquiry reports on child deaths in more recent years have continued to press home social workers' responsibility for child protection, rather than family support. More elaborate guidance for interagency practice has been produced (Home Office et al 1991) and a growing body of specialist social workers has gone into action to make sure the procedures are faithfully carried out.

What is harder to find is a clear statement of the aims of the child protection system: what is it trying to achieve *beyond* applying the approved procedures? The emphasis of the procedures is on identification of children at risk. Inter-agency co-ordinative mechanisms are intended to prevent children in danger from slipping through the protective net. The unstated fear behind the procedures may be that another child will be killed. Yet this is a comparatively rare event that can probably never be successfully predicted. This may be why there is apparently little change in children's death rates from homicide over the last fifteen years in spite of the growth of the system and the increasing rate of children placed on registers for inter-agency protection (NSPCC, 1992). The ever-present fear of serious or fatal injury to a child may explain why the social workers in this study concentrated on surveillance and monitoring to ensure children's physical safety. They appeared to pay less attention to warning signs of distorted socio-emotional development and low achievement. If the goals of the system were more clearly defined to give higher priority to the promotion of welfare and children's longer-term normal development, the pattern of intervention might change.

In this study, we could find no evidence that children who were legally protected (by care or other orders) did significantly better. Nor did those removed from their abusers, and placed in new permanent or long-term families, have significantly better behavioural outcomes than those who remained with their original carers. This still held, even for children who had been in their new families almost from the start of their lives and had not experienced many moves. This may have been due to poor selection of children for placement – although the children in new families had a greater weighting of risk factors than the others, the differences were small. Contemporary policies may also have interpreted the need for 'permanency' in an over-restrictive way.

However, the findings also suggested that one could not guarantee a better quality of parenting simply by moving a child to a non-abusing family. Apparently harmful parenting methods, notably the use of physical punishment in a generally punitive atmosphere, were found about as often in adoptive homes as in natural families – though not in foster homes. Foster carers had ongoing support from social workers which adoptive parents usually lacked. The need for further development of post-adoptive work was highlighted.

The Children Act (1989) calls for a new approach in social work with children and families. A fundamental principle is that the primary responsibility for bringing up children should rest with their parents. The state should be ready to help parents discharge that responsibility (through family support provision) and should only intervene compulsorily in very restricted circumstances. A care or supervision order must not be made in respect of a child unless the court considers that doing so would be better for the child than making no order at all. Social workers will have to carry out better assessments, and be able to demonstrate convincingly that compulsory intervention in family life is likely to produce benefits for the child.

Parents have more rights to information and to be consulted at all stages of the child protection process. They should be present at meetings where the nature of intervention is discussed and decided. If problems likely to affect children's development are to be tackled, parents' agreement and understanding will have to be won. This presents an opportunity to alert parents to observed problems in child development, family relationships or parenting style, and to link them with sources of help in the community. Help needs to be more directly geared to children's developmental needs and more priority should be given to developing direct treatment services for them. The evidence from this study suggested that children may need particular help in learning how to make satisfying relationships with others of their own age. Social groupwork, sadly under-developed in training and practice in this country, could perhaps have a useful contribution to make here. Children also often needed help in adjusting to the school environment, but advice on management from educationists was rarely found.

The child protection system has succeeded in fostering inter-agency co-ordination in the early stages of identification and registration, but inter-professional co-ordination is much less evident in the effort to help the child and family (Hallett & Birchall, 1992). Policy changes would be needed to increase the access of abused children and their families to sources of educational and psychological help, and to enable more social workers to acquire specific therapeutic skills.

Help for abused children appeared to be more effective when the key social worker took an active role in co-ordinating a broadly-based package of services, focused on specific problems, that included help from a voluntary agency or a family centre. Large-scale research into the effectiveness of services for abused children in the US also demonstrated the value of including lay helpers in treatment programmes (Cohn & Daro, 1987). Demonstration projects might provide a means of developing this form of service delivery and evaluating its effectiveness in different circumstances.

References

ABER, J.L and CICCHETTI, D. (1984) The socioemotional development of maltreated children: an empirical and theoretical analysis. In Fitzgerald, H. and Yogman, M. (Eds.) *Theory and Research in Behavioural Pediatrics Vol II.* New York: Plenum

ABER, J.L. et al., (1989) Effects of maltreatment on development during early childhood: recent studies and their theoretical, clinical and policy implications. In Cicchetti, D. and Carlson, V. (Eds.) *Child Maltreatment: Theory and Research on the Causes and Consequences of Child Abuse and Neglect,* Cambridge: Cambridge University Press

ADAMS, M. and ADAMS, J. (1991) Life events, depression and perceived problem solving alternatives in adolescents. *Journal of Child Psychology and Psychiatry,* **32**, 811–820

ADAMS-TUCKER, C. (1982) Proximate effects of sexual abuse in childhood: a report on 28 children. *American Journal of Psychiatry,* **139**, 1252–1256

AUGOUSTINOS, M. (1987) Developmental effects of child abuse: recent findings. *Child Abuse and Neglect,* **11**, 15–27

ALLEN, R.E. and OLIVER, J.M. (1982) The effects of child maltreatment on language development. *Child Abuse and Neglect,* **6**, 299–305

BAGLEY, C.R. (1990) Measuring child sexual abuse and its long-term psychological outcomes: a review of some British and Canadian studies of victims and their families. *Paper presented to the Eighth International Congress on Child Abuse and Neglect, Hamburg,* September 1990

BARRERA, M. (1981) Social support in the adjustment of pregnant adolescents: assessment issues. In Gottlieb, B.H. (Ed.) *Social Networks and Social Support.* Beverly Hills: Sage

BARRERA, M. (1985) Informant corroboration of social network data, *Connections,* **8**, 9–13

BERDEN, G.F.M.G., ALTHOUSS, M. and VERHULST, F.C. (1990) Major life events and changes in the behaviour functioning of children. *Journal of Child Psychology and Psychiatry,* **31**, 949–959

BIRLESON, P. (1981) The validity of depressive disorder in childhood and the development of a self-rating scale: a research report. *Journal of Child Psychology and Psychiatry,* **22**, 73–88

BRADSHAW, J. (1990) *Child Poverty and Deprivation in the UK.* London: National Children's Bureau

BROWN, G.W. and HARRIS, T. (1978) *The Social Origins of Depression.* London: Tavistock

CAFFEY, J. (1972) On the theory and practice of shaking infants: its potential residual effects of permanent brain damage and mental retardation. *American Journal of Diseases of Children,* **124**, 161–169

CALAM, R. and FRANCHI, C. (1987) *Child Abuse and its Consequences: Observational Approaches.* Cambridge: Cambridge University Press

CAPLAN, G. (Ed.) (1974) *Support Systems and Community Mental Health.* New York: Basic Books

COHN, A.H. and DARO, D. (1987) Is treatment too late: what ten years of evaluative research tells us. *Child Abuse and Neglect,* **11**, 433–442

CLAUSSEN, A.H. and CRITTENDEN, P.M. (1991) Physical and psychological maltreatment: relation among types of maltreatment, *Child Abuse and Neglect,* **15**, 5–18

CORBY, B. (1987) *Working with Child Abuse: Social Work Practice and the Child Abuse System.* Milton Keynes: Open University Press

CORDRAY, S. AND POLK, K. (1983) The implications of respondent loss in panel studies of deviant behaviour. *Journal of Research in Crime and Delinquency,* **20**, 214–242

COX, A., POUND, A. & PUCKERING, C. (1992) NEWPIN: a befriending scheme and therapeutic network for carers of young children. In Gibbons, J. (Ed.) *The Children Act 1989 and Family Support: Principles into Practice.* London: HMSO

CREIGHTON, S.J. (1985) An epidemiological study of abused children and their families in the UK, *Child Abuse and Neglect,* **9**, 441–448

CREIGHTON, S.J. and NOYES P. (1989) *Child Abuse Trends in England and Wales 1983–1987.* London: NSPCC

CRONBACH, L.J. (1951) Coefficient alpha and the internal structure of tests, *Psychometrika,* **16**, 297–334

Department of Health (1991 a) *Children and Young Persons on Child Protection Registers Year Ending 31 March 1990 England.* London: Department of Health

Department of Health (1991 b) *Children in Care of Local Authorities Year Ending 31 March 1990 England and Wales.* London: Department of Health

Department of Health (1993) *Children and Young People on Child Protection Registers Year Ending 31 March 1992 England.* London: Department of Health

DUNN, L.M., WHETTON C. and PINTILIE, D. (1982) *The British Picture Vocabulary Scale.* Windsor: NFER-NELSON Publishing Company Ltd.

EGELAND, B. and SROUFE, L.A. (1981) Developmental sequelae of maltreatment in infancy. In R. Rizley and D. Cicchetti (Eds), *New Directions in Child Development: Developmental Perspectives in Child Maltreatment*. San Francisco: Jossey-Bass

EGELAND, B. SROUFE, L.A. and ERICKSON, M. (1983) The developmental consequences of different patterns of maltreatment. *Child Abuse and Neglect*, **7**, 459–469

EGELAND, B., JACOBVITZ, D. and PAPATOLA, K. (1984) Intergenerational continuity of abuse, *Paper presented at the Social Science Research Council Conference on Child Abuse and Neglect*, York, Maine

ELLIOTT, D.C., MURRAY, D.J. and PEARSON, L.S. (1983) *British Ability Scales* (Revised Edition). NFER – Nelson Publishing Company Ltd., Windsor

ELMER, E. (1967) *Children in Jeopardy: A Study of Abused Minors and their Families*. Pittsburgh: Pittsburgh University Press

ELMER, E. (1977) *Fragile Families Troubled Children*. Pittsburgh: University Press

ELMER, E., GRACE, S. and GREGG M.D. (1967) Developmental characteristics of abused children. *Pediatrics*, **40**, 596–602

ERICKSON, M.F., EGELAND, B. & PIANTA, R. (1989) The effects of maltreatment on the development of young children. In D. Cichetti & V. Carlson eds. *Child Maltreatment: Theory and Research on the Causes and Consequences of Child Abuse and Neglect*. Cambridge: Cambridge University Press

FABER, E.E. and EGELAND, B. (1987) Invulnerability among abused and neglected children. In: Anthony, E.J. and Cohler, B.J. (Eds.) *The Invulnerable Child*. London: The Guildford Press

FARMER, E. and PARKER, R. (1991) *Trials and Tribulations: Returning Children from Local Authority Care to their Families*. London: HMSO

FARMER, E. and OWEN, M. (1993) *Decision-making, Intervention and Outcome in Child Protection Work*. University of Bristol: Report to Department of Health

FINKLEHOR, D. (1984) *Child Sexual Abuse: New Theory and Research*. New York: Free Press

FROMUTH, M.E. (1986) The relationship of childhood abuse with later psychological and sexual adjustment in a sample of college women. *Child Abuse and Neglect*, **10**, 5–15

GARMEZY, N. and RUTTER M. (1983) *Stress, Coping and Development in Children*. McGraw-Hill

GEORGE, C. and MAIN, M. (1979) Social interactions of young abused children: approach, avoidance, and aggression. *Child Development,* **50,** 306–318

GIBBONS, J., THORPE, S. and WILKINSON, P. (1990) *Family Support and Prevention: Studies in Local Areas.* London: HMSO

GIBBONS, J., CONROY, S. and BELL, C. (1994) *Operation of Child Protection Registers.* London: HMSO

GIL, D.G. (1970) *Violence Against Children: Physical Child Abuse in the United States.* Cambridge: Harvard University Press

GOTTLIEB, B.H. (1983) *Social Support Strategies: Guidelines for Mental Health.* Beverly Hills: Sage

GOUGH, D.A. BODDY, E.A., DUNNING, N. and STONE, F.H. (1987) *A Longitudinal Study of Child Abuse in Glasgow, Vol 1, The Children who were Registered.* Report to Social Work Services Group, Scottish Office

GOUGH, D.A., TAYLOR, J.P. and BODDY, F.A. (1988) *Child Abuse Interventions: A Review of the Research Literature.* Glasgow: Glasgow University Press

GRAY, E. (1988) The link between child abuse and juvenile delinquency: what we know and recommendations for policy. In Hotaling G.T. et al (Eds.) *Family Abuse and Its Consequences.* Beverly Hills: Sage

GRAY, J., CUTLER, C., DEAN, J. and KEMPE, C.H. (1976) Perinatal observations. In Helfer, R.E. and Kempe, C.H. (Eds.) *Child Abuse and Neglect. The Family and the Community.* Cambridge, Mass: Ballinger

GREEN, A. (1978) Psychiatric treatment of the abused child. *Journal of the American Academy of Child Psychiatry,* 17, 356

GREGORY, H.M. and BEVERIDGE, M.C. (1984) The social and emotional adjustment of abused children. *Child Abuse and Neglect,* **8,** 525–531

HALLETT, C. and BIRCHALL, E. (1992) *Coordination and Child Protection: A Review of the Literature.* Edinburgh: HMSO

HARDING, L.F. (1991) *Perspectives in Child Care Policy.* London: Longman

HENSEY, O.J., WILLIAMS, J.K. & ROSENBLOOM, L. (1983) Intervention in child abuse: experience in Liverpool. *Developmental Medicine and Child Neurology,* **25,** 606–611

HOLMES, T.H. and RAHE, R.H. (1967) The social readjustment rating scale. *Journal of Psychosomatic Research,* **11,** 213–218

Home Office et al. (1991) *Working Together Under the Children Act 1989.* London: HMSO

HOWE, D. (1992) Assessing adoptions in difficulty. *British Journal of Social Work,* 22, 1–15

HYMAN, C.A. and PARR, R. (1978) A controlled video observation study of abused children. *Child Abuse and Neglect*, **2**, 217–222

JACOBSON, R.S. and STRAKER, G. (1982) Peer group interaction of physically abused children. *Child Abuse and Neglect*, **6**, 321–327

JAFFE, P., WOLFE, D., WILEEN, S. and ZAK, L. (1986) Similarities in behavioral and social maladjustment among child victims and witnesses to family violence. *American Journal of Orthopsychiatry*, **56**, 142–146

KEMPE, C.H., SILVERMAN, F.N., STEELE, B.F., et al., (1962) The battered child syndrome. *Journal of the American Medical Association.*, **181**, 17–24

KINARD, E.M. (1980) Emotional development in physically abused children. *American Journal of Orthopsychiatry*, **50**, 686–696

LAMPHEAR, V.S. (1985) The impact of maltreatment on children: psychosocial adjustment: a review of the research. *Child Abuse and Neglect*, **9**, 251–263

LAMPHEAR, V.S. (1986) The psychological adjustment of maltreated children: methodological limitations and guidelines for future research. *Child Abuse and Neglect*, **10**, 63–69

LAWDER, E.A. et al. (1984) *Helping the Multi-Problem Family, A Study of Services to Children in their own Homes.* Children's Aid Society of Pennsylvania

LYNCH, M.A. (1978) The follow-up of abused children – a researcher's nightmare. In Eekelaar, J.M. and Kate, S.M. (Eds.) *Family Violence: An International and Interdisciplinary Study.* London: Butterworth

LYNCH, M.A. and ROBERTS, J. (1982) *Consequences of Child Abuse.* London: Academic Press

McCORD, J. (1978) A thirty-year follow-up of treatment effect. *American Psychologist*, **33**, 284–289

McFARLANE, A.C. (1988) Recent life events and psychiatric disorder in children: the interaction with preceding extreme adversity. *Journal of Child Psychology and Psychiatry*, **29**, 677–690

MAGURA, S. and MOSES, B.S. (1984) Clients as evaluators in child protection services. *Child Welfare*, **53**, 99–112

MARTIN, H.P., BEEZLEY, P., CONWAY, E.F. and KEMPE, H. (1974) The development of abused children. *Advances in Pediatrics*, 21, 25–73

MARTIN, H.P., (Ed.) (1979) *The Abused Child: a multi-disciplinary approach to developmental issues.* Cambridge, Mass.: Ballinger

MAUGHAN, B. and PICKLES, A. (1990) Adopted and illegitimate children growing up. In Robins, L.N. and Rutter, M. *Straight and Devious Pathways from Childhood to Adulthood.* Cambridge: Cambridge University Press

MORSE, C.W. SAHLER, O.J. and FREIDMAN, S.B. (1970) A follow-up of abused and neglected children. *American Journal of Diseases of Children*, **120**, 439–446

MURPHY, M. (1990) Minimizing attrition in longitudinal research: means or ends? In: Magnusson, D. and Bergman, L.R. (Eds.) *Data Quality in Longitudinal Research*. Cambridge: Cambridge University Press

NAKOU, S., ADAM, H., STATHACOPOULON, K. and AGATHONOS, H. (1982) Health status of abused and neglected children and their siblings. *Child Abuse and Neglect*, **6**, 279–284

National Children's Home (1990) *Survey of Treatment Facilities for Abused Children and Of Treatment Facilities for Young Sexual Abusers of Children*. London: NCH

National Society for the Prevention of Cruelty to Children (1992) *Child Abuse Deaths: Information Briefing Number 5 (Revised)*. London: NSPCC

NICOL, A.R., SMITH, J., KAY, B., HALL, D., BARLOW, J. and WILLIAMS, B. (1988) A focused casework approach to the treatment of child abuse: a controlled comparison. *Journal of Child Psychology and Psychiatry*, **29**, 703–711

NUNNALLY, J.C. (1978) *Psychometric Theory*. New Delhi: Tata McGraw Hill

OATES, R.K. (1984a) Personality development after physical abuse. *Archives of Disease in Childhood*, **59**, 147–150

OATES, R.K., PEACOCK, A. and FOREST, D. (1984b) The development of abused children. *Developmental Medicine and Child Neurology*, **26**, 649–656

OATES, R.K., FOREST, D. and PEACOCK, A. (1985) Self-esteem of abused children, 9, 159–163

OLLENDICK, T.H. (1983) Reliability and validity of the Revised Fear Survey Schedule for Children (FSSC-R). *Behaviour Research and Therapy*, **21**, 685–692

PARISH, R.A., MYERS, P.A., BRANDER, A. and TEMPLIN, K.H. (1985) Developmental milestones in abused children and their improvements with family-orientated approach to the treatment of child abuse. *Child Abuse and Neglect*, **9**, 245–250

PATTERSON, G.R. (1982) *Coercive Family Processes*. Eugene OR: Castalia

PEARLIN, L.I. (1985) Social structure and processes of social support. In Cohen, S. and Syme, S.L. *Social Support and Health*. London: Academic Press

RAVEN, J.C., COURT, J.H. and RAVEN, J. (1976) *Raven's Progressive Matrices*. London: H.K. Lewis Co. Ltd.

REID, J. TAPLIN, P. and LARBER, R. (1981) A social interactional approach to the treatment of abusive families. In: Stuart, K. (Ed.) *Violent Behavior: Social Learning Approaches to Prediction, Management and Treatment*. New York: Brunner/Mazel

RODEHEFFER, M. and MARTIN, H.P. (1976) Special problems in the developmental assessment of abused children. In: Martin, H.P. and Rodeheffer, M. (Eds.) *The Abused Child: A multi-disciplinary approach to developmental issues and treatment*. Cambridge, Mass: Ballinger

ROGOWSKI, S. and McGRATH, M. (1986) United we stand up to the pressures that lead to child abuse. *Social Work Today*, **17**, 13–14

RUNYAN, D.K. and GOULD, C.L. (1985) Foster care for child maltreatment: impact on delinquent behavior. *Pediatrics*, **75**, 562

RUSHTON, A., TRESEDER, J. & QUINTON, D. (1993) New Parents for Older Children: Support Services during 8 Years of Placement. *Adoption & Fostering*, in press

RUTTER, M. (1967) A children's behaviour questionnaire for completion by teachers: preliminary findings. *Journal of Child Psychology and Psychiatry*, **8**, 1–11

RUTTER, M. (1981) Stress, coping and development: some issues and questions. *Journal of Child Psychology and Psychiatry*, **22**, 323–356

RUTTER, M., TIZARD, J. and WHITMORE, K. (1970) *Education, Health and Behaviour*. London: Longman

RUTTER, M. and GARMEZY, N. (1983) Developmental psychopathology. In Hetherington, E.M. (Ed.) *Handbook of Child Psychology Vol 4*. Chichester: Wiley

RUTTER, M., QUINTON, D. and HILL, J. (1990) Adult outcomes of institution-reared children: males and females compared. In Robins, L.N. and Rutter, M. (Eds.) *Straight and Devious Pathways from Childhood to Adulthood*. Cambridge: Cambridge University Press

SANDLER, I.N. and BLOCK, M. (1979) Life stress and maladaption of children. *American Journal of Community Psychology*, **8**, 41–52

SINCLAIR, I., personal communication

SKINNER, A.E. and CASTLE, R.L. (1969) *Eight Severely Battered Children: A Retrospective Study*. London: NSPCC

SPEIGHT, A.N.P., BRIDSON, J.M. and COOPER, C.E. (1979) Follow-up of cases of child abuse seen at Newcastle General Hospital 1974–75. *Child Abuse and Neglect*, **3**, 555–563

STEEH, C.G. (1981) Trends in non-response rates, 1956–1979. *Public Opinion Quarterly*, **45**, 46–57

STEPHENSON, P.S. (1977) Reaching child abusers through target toddlers. *Victimology*, **2**, 310–316

STONE, N.M. and STONE, S.F. (1983) The prediction of successful foster placement. *Social Casework*, **64**, 11–17

STOTT, D.H. (1974) *The Social Adjustment of Children* (4th Ed.) London: University of London Press

SWEARINGEN, E.M. and COHEN, L.H. (1985) Life events and psychological distress: a prospective study of young adolescents. *Developmental Psychology*, **21**, 1045–1054

THOBURN, J. (1990) *Review of Research Relating to Adoption: Interdepartmental Review of Adoption Law: Background Paper No. 2*. London: Department of Health

THOBURN, J. and ROWE, J. (1988) A snapshot of permanent substitute family placement. *Adoption and Fostering*, **12** (3), 29–34

THOMAS, A. and CHESS, S. (1984) Genesis and evolution of behavioural disorders from infancy to early adult life. *American Journal of Psychiatry*, **141**, 1–9

TORO, P.A. (1982) Developmental effects of child abuse: recent findings. *Child Abuse and Neglect*, **11**, 15–27

VAUX, A. and RUGGIERO, M. (1983) Stressful life changes and delinquent behaviour. *American Journal of Community Psychology*, **11**, 169–183

WEIR, K. and DUVEEN, G. (1981) Further development and validation of the Prosocial behaviour Questionnaire for use by teachers. *Journal of Child Psychology and Psychiatry*, **22**, 357–374

WEST, D.J. and FARRINGTON, D.P.F. (1973) *Who Becomes Delinquent*. London: Heinemann

WIDOM, C.S. (1989) The cycle of violence. *Science*, **244**, 160–166

WODARSKI, J.S., KURTZ, P.D., GAUDIN, J.M. & HOVING, P.T. (1990) Maltreatment and the school-age child: major academic, socioemotional and adaptive outcomes. *Social Work*, **35**, 506–513

WOLFE, D.A. (1987) Child abuse: implications for child development and psychopathology. *Developmental Clinical Psychology and Psychiatry*, **10**

WOLFE, D.A., SANDLER, J. and KAUFMAN, K. (1981) A competency-based parent training program for child abusers. *Journal of Consulting and Clinical Psychology*, **49**, 633–640

WOLFGANG, M.E., THORNBERRY, T.P. & FIGLIO, R.M. (1987) *From Boys to Men, From Delinquency to Crime*. Chicago: University of Chicago Press

Name index

Index

Appendices

Report of statistical consultancy
B. Everitt, Sigma X Consultancy

1. Introduction

The Family Health and Development Project is a three year study, sponsored by the Department of Health. The two main aims of the project were as follows:

1. To document the 10 year outcome of children placed on child protection registers after physical abuse, who were exposed to different kinds of protective intervention.

2. To compare the behaviour and achievements of the abused children with those of similar children who had not been physically abused.

A total of 288 children, 144 in the Index group and 144 in the Comparison group were studied. Initially each child in the Index sample was matched with a Comparison child. This matching is, however, ignored in the analysis described in this report. The aim of the analysis carried out by Sigma X was to find some ways of combining and summarising the outcome measures to provide a useful and informative 'outcome profile' for each child.

2. Analysis

Initially several principle component analyses were performed on a variety of sub-sets of the variables in the outcome data. Here we report the results of the analysis which led to the composite outcome scores used in the next stage of the investigation.

The outcome variables used in the analysis are listed in Table 3 and their correlation matrix is given in Table 4. A total of 257 children had complete data on these variables. The results of the principal components analysis are summarised in Table 5. The first four components had eigenvalues greater than one and it is these which form the basis of the suggested 'outcome profile'.

The interpretation of the four components is relatively straightforward:

- Component 1 – Parent's rating of behaviour problems – PARB
- Component 2 – Performance score – PERFSC
- Component 3 – Teachers' rating of behaviour problems – TEACHB
- Component 4 – Fear and depression score – FDEPSC

Next the score of each child on each of the four components described above was found, and these scores subjected to a 'k-means' cluster analysis (see

Everitt, 1980). A summary of the 3 group solution is given in Table 6. Clearly the first cluster contains those children whose outcome is very poor; they have high scores on parents' ratings of behaviour problems, a low perform-ance score, and above average scores on both teacher problem ratings and the fear/depression score. Cluster two on the other hand, contains those children having a good outcome – low parent and teacher ratings of behaviour problems, a high performance score and low fear/depression score. Cluster three appears to be an intermediate group, containing children who have high teacher ratings of their behaviour problems but relatively low parent ratings, low performance and averge fear/depression scores.

Cross-tabulating cluster membership against whether the child was from the Index or Comparison sample gives the following results.

Sample	Cluster 1	Cluster 2	Cluster 3
Index	54	28	47
Comparison	25	61	42

The Index group are clearly over-represented in the cluster identified with poor outcome, although it is of interest to note that a substantial number of these children are assigned to the cluster having a good outcome. An equal number of Index and Comparison children appear in cluster 3.

Finally t-tests were made of the differences between the Index and Comparison groups on each of the outcome measures; these are reported in Table 7. There are clear differences between the Index and Comparison samples on the four outcome measures.

Table 1   **Child outcome measures**

Children's Behaviour

1. Scores on Rutter A Questionnaire (parent information)
   (i) Hyperactivity
   (ii) Conduct disorder
   (iii) Emotional disorder
   (iv) Total A score

2. Scores on Rutter B Questionnaire (teacher information)
   (i) Antisocial score
   (ii) Neurotic score
   (iii) Total B score

3. Children's self-report
   (i) Depression questionnaire
   (ii) Fears questionnaire
   (iii) Peer relationships

Children's Cognitive Development
   (i) IQ
   (ii) Scores on standardised tests of language and number

Table 2 **Current family circumstances**

1. Child race
2. Single parent
3. Disadvantage score
4. Social class
5. Parental violence
6. Area
7. Parental involvement
8. Parent control
9. Partner status
10. Time together
11. Social contact
12. Marital problems
13. Money problems
14. Parent/Child
15. Health
16. Respondent violence
17. Partner violence
18. Partner conflict
19. Nerves
20. Child nerves
21. Social Security
22. Main carer malaise
23. Social work contact
24. Child's sex

Table 3 **Outcome measures used in investigation to define outcome profile**

1. Ravens raw score
2. BPVS standardised score
3. BAS similarities T score
4. BAS number skill T score
5. BAS word reading T scores
6. Total behaviour score (parent)
7. Disorder threshold (parent)
8. Emotion score (parent)
9. Conduct score (parent)
10. Hyperactivity score (parent)
11. Depression score (child)
12. Fears score (child)
13. Total behaviour score (teacher)
14. Disorder threshold (teacher)
15. Neurotic score (teacher)
16. Antisocial score (teacher)

Table 4 **Correlations between outcome variables listed in Table 3**

	1	2	3	4	5	6	7	8	9	10	11	12	13	14	15	16
1	1.00															
2	0.42	1.00														
3	0.44	0.55	1.00													
4	0.45	0.50	0.51	1.00												
5	0.41	0.51	0.48	0.51	1.00											
6	−0.29	−0.18	−0.28	−0.36	−0.25	1.00										
7	−0.25	−0.16	−0.23	−0.33	−0.20	0.79	1.00									
8	−0.07	−0.05	−0.11	−0.16	−0.09	0.64	0.44	1.00								
9	−0.30	−0.22	−0.26	−0.35	−0.30	0.79	0.63	0.31	1.00							
10	−0.33	−0.17	−0.25	−0.31	−0.15	0.70	0.53	0.31	0.51	1.00						
11	−0.05	−0.13	−0.07	−0.16	−0.12	0.24	0.21	0.15	0.30	0.11	1.00					
12	−0.12	−0.18	−0.18	−0.15	−0.09	0.19	0.16	0.08	0.15	0.09	0.36	1.00				
13	−0.27	−0.28	−0.20	−0.33	−0.31	0.45	0.31	0.25	0.41	0.33	0.16	0.12	1.00			
14	−0.22	−0.18	−0.15	−0.27	−0.21	0.38	0.26	0.21	0.34	0.31	0.17	0.17	0.83	1.00		
15	−014	−014	−0.09	−021	−0.2	0.26	0.17	0.18	0.18	0.19	0.13	0.16	0.63	0.50	1.00	
16	−0.22	−0.27	−0.17	−0.26	−0.26	0.38	0.26	0.19	0.40	0.25	0.09	0.04	0.81	0.66	0.17	1.00

Table 5 **Results of Principal Components Analysis on Outcome Measures**

Variable	PC1	PC2	PC3	PC4
Beh. Sc. (Par.)	0.92	0.00	0.00	0.00
Dis. Th. (Par)	0.82	0.00	0.00	0.00
Con. Sc. (Par)	0.74	0.00	0.00	0.00
Hyp. Sc. (Par)	0.71	0.00	0.00	0.00
Emt. Sc. (Par)	0.66	0.00	0.00	0.00
Beh. Sc. (Tch)	0.00	0.00	0.93	0.00
Dis. Th. (Tch)	0.00	0.00	0.87	0.00
Ant. Sc. (Tch)	0.00	0.00	0.76	0.00
Neu. Sc. (Tch)	0.00	0.00	0.64	0.00
BAS. Sim (T)	0.00	0.78	0.00	0.00
BPV Stan. Sc.	0.00	0.78	0.00	0.00
BAS Bsc (T)	0.00	0.73	0.00	0.00
RAV. Rsc.	0.00	0.67	0.00	0.00
BAS. Wrd. (T)	0.00	0.75	0.00	0.00
Fear (Ch.)	0.00	0.00	0.00	0.80
Dep. (Ch.)	0.00	0.00	0.00	0.78
Variance	3.32	3.04	2.85	1.41

Note Sorted Rotated Loadings after Varimax rotation (Loadings less than 0.25 have been replaced by zero)

Table 6 **Cluster analysis results**

Cluster		Outcome Measure			
		PARBP	**PERFSC**	**TEACHBP**	**FDEPSC**
1 (n=79)	Mean	4.80	−1.44	0.46	0.58
	SD	2.94	2.85	3.36	1.73
2 (n=89)	Mean	−2.34	3.91	−0.70	−0.85
	SD	2.12	2.47	3.23	1.23
3 (n=89)	Mean	−1.86	−2.21	0.56	0.29
	SD	2.18	2.44	3.42	1.67

Table 7 **Tests to compare Index and Comparison samples on four derived outcome measures**

Outcome measure		Index	Compar.	*t*	*p*
PARBP	Mean	0.91	−0.89	3.94	0.0001
	SD	4.24	3.48		
	n	144	144		
PERFSC	Mean	−0.76	0.72	−3.18	0.002
	SD	3.60	4.07		
	n	138	136		
TEACHBP	Mean	0.86	−0.84	4.33	0.0001
	SD	3.51	2.94		
	n	137	136		
PDEPSC	Mean	0.17	−0.17	1.76	0.08
	SD	1.60	1.68		
	n	136	140		

Ethical Guidelines for the conduct of the study

1. Introduction

The Family Health and Development Project (FHDP) is a follow-up study of 170 children who were abused or at risk and whose names were put on child protection registers about 10 years ago. All the children were under the age of 5 years at the time of registration. The aims of the study are: to increase knowledge of the long-term effects of child abuse; to evaluate the effect of various professional interventions with abused children; to describe the 'careers' of abused children. The means by which this will be done is a study of official records (voluntary agency files, social service files, school records, hospital files and GP records). Interviews will be conducted with the registered children and their carers.

Through this research it should ultimately be possible to make recommendations as to how both professional practice and official policy, pertaining to a variety of disciplines, can be improved. Practitioners and researchers have a duty to maximise the quality of services to clients and also to identify practices which may be harmful to their long-term welfare. It is the stated view of the research team and its Central Advisory Committee that not to undertake this type of research would in itself be unethical.

While there is an ethical responsibility to conduct research into services for abused children, there is an equal responsibility that any such research should itself be conducted according to the strictest ethical rules. The Ethical Guidelines upon which this research will be based are given in detail below, but the main principles are: 1) no aspect of this research should directly or indirectly cause any distress to any individual or group of individuals; 2) data should be afforded the maximum of confidentiality and security at all times; 3) permission must be sought from the relevant authority before searching any official record and any rules laid down by any of these authorities must be adhered to; and 4) in the event of any conflict between the needs of this research and the work of any practitioner then the latter should always assume priority.

The FHDP does not know the present whereabouts of any of the children's current carers/legal guardians. This makes it impossible to ask them for their permission to search any record. In fact it is only by a search of official records that the project will be able to trace the children or their carers/legal guardians. One of the major questions to be addressed by this study is whether registered children can be traced after so many years. The vast majority of tracing must depend upon official records.

Once the children and their carers/legal guardians have been traced then the project will not proceed to any further stage of the study ie. interviews and questionnaires, without gaining consent of the legal guardians. However, at no time will the legal guardian be told that this is a study of child abuse. Not only would this be potentially distressing to them but it may also be a breach of confidentiality.

The FDHP research team is supported by a Central Advisory Committee chaired by Professor Sir Michael Rutter. The CAC was set up to give advice on theoretical, methodological and ethical issues. It includes representatives from the Department of Health, the Association of Directors of Social Services and the NSPCC. Also sitting on the committee are consultant paediatricians and a number of researchers drawn from both University and Hospital Departments.

2.   Contact with caregivers/legal guardians

(i)   Before conducting any interview with a child or a carer, permission will be sought from the child's legal guardian, who will be asked to sign a consent form (specimen consent form attached).

(ii)   No carer/legal guardian will be approached directly. Rather they will be sent a letter (specimen letter attached) from the FHDP outlining the nature of the project and pointing out that a Research Officer will visit them in order to explain the project more fully and to invite them to take part.

(iii)   Correspondence sent to carers/legal guardians will not carry any information that could have a labelling effect for that person or for the subject child – this applies to both the envelope and the message contained inside. Furthermore the letter will be written in such a way that it will not elicit any anxiety in the subject as to the nature of the research project.

(iv)   Index children will not be distinguished from the control children in any way. When answering queries as to how the children were selected, the researcher will say that they were chosen on the basis that they were in a certain age group and that their names were on one of the lists of a number of child-based services for both healthy children and children with problems.

3.   Permission

(i)   Before obtaining information from a child's school record the FHDP will have sought and gained the permission of the Local Education Authority and the individual Head Teacher.

(ii) Before searching a child's Social Services file the FHDP will have sought and gained the permission of the Social Services Department.

(iii) Before searching a child's hospital file the FHDP will have sought and gained permission from the responsible medical ethical committee and consultant if necessary.

(iv) The above procedures will be followed, as appropriate, before searches are carried out on any other official record. Furthermore, the research team is aware that permission given by any of the above agencies in the two study areas will not serve as permission in any other local authority area. Therefore permission will be sought and gained on an individual authority basis, although it is hoped that clearance by a given agency in one authority will make acceptance by the same agency in a different authority easier.

4.   Research procedure

(i) The title by which the study is to be known will not have any particular connotations, especially negative ones. The title will not make any reference to child abuse and no such reference will be made when describing the project unless it is necessary. The study will, at all times, be referred to as the Family Health and Development Project.

(ii) The address of the FHDP will not have any particular connotations, especially negative ones.

(iii) Papers describing the project will exist in two forms: one is a comprehensive version which will refer to child abuse and will be available to those persons giving permission for record searches and also to fellow researchers. The second is a summarised version which does not refer to child abuse. This paper is designed and is intended for these professionals who work with a subject.

(iv) When engaged in personal contact members of the research team will refer to the study as being a follow-up of children who have had contact with child based services eg. health visitors, schools and paediatricians. No reference will be made to child abuse, the NSPCC or that a given child has been in contact with any particular service.

(v) Practitioners and other researchers who come into contact with this project and who are aware of its precise nature will be expected to adhere to the Ethical Guidelines.

(vi) Any general publicity concerning this research will not refer to the children having been on registers in any particular area. Papers published in academic journals will refer to the sample as being register-based.

5.   Confidentiality

(i)   Data from this project will not be released to any person or organisation not directly related to it.

(ii)   Individual persons and organisations will not be identified or identifiable through this research.

(iii)   Data from this project will be kept in a locked cabinet in a locked room unless they are being worked on. Transportation of data will be kept to an absolute minimum and will be undertaken with the strictest security.

(iv)   Storage and communication of data will be governed not only by the Ethical Guidelines but also by the researchers' individual contracts, conditions laid down by participatory organisations, and by any relevant legislation eg. Data Protection Act and Official Secrets Act (criminal records).

(v)   At the end of the study period, the research team will carry out any instructions laid down by organisations participating in the research which concern the return, destruction, or otherwise of official records.

6.   General

(i)   This research project has received approval from the ACPC in each study area, and from the DHSS Children's Research Liaison Group.

(ii)   In drawing up the Ethical Guidelines, the research team sought the advice of the CAC and the NSPCC. Advice has also been received from individual practitioners and researchers.

(iii)   The Ethical Guidelines will be reviewed on a regular basis with the assistance of the CAC and the Local Liaison Committees (LLC) which are to be set up. (The LLC consists of representatives from Social Service, Education, Health and the NSPCC. Its function is to facilitate access to records and provide local knowledge).

(iv)   The Child Abuse Policy Committee in each study area will receive regular reports concerning the progress of the FHDP.

(v)   The Research Officer will be available to answer any queries from organisations participating in the research.

Forthcoming complementary studies include:

Parental Perspectives in Cases of Suspected Child Abuse
Hedy Cleaver and Pam Freeman (The Dartington Team)
HMSO, 1995, ISBN 0 11 321786 2

Child Protection Practice: Private Risks and Public Remedies
Elaine Farmer and Morag Owen (The University of Bristol Team)
HMSO, 1995, ISBN 0 11 321787 0

The Prevalence of Child Sexual Abuse in Britain
Deborah Ghate and Liz Spencer (Social and Community Planning Research)
HMSO, 1995, ISBN 0 11 321783 8

Operating the Child Protection System
Jane Gibbons, Sue Conroy and Caroline Bell (University of East Anglia)
HMSO, 1995, ISBN 0 11 321785 4

Inter-agency Coordination and Child Protection
Christine Hallett (The University of Stirling)
HMSO, 1995, ISBN 0 11 321789 7

Working Together in Child Protection
Elizabeth Birchall (The University of Stirling)
HMSO, 1995, ISBN 0 11 321830 3

Paternalism or Partnership? Family Involvement in the Child Protection Process
June Thoburn, Ann Lewis and David Shemmings (University of East Anglia)
HMSO, 1995, ISBN 0 11 321788 9

Printed in the United Kingdom for HMSO
Dd300756 2/95 C7 G539 10170